Samuel Smith Harris

The Dignity of Man

Select Sermons

Samuel Smith Harris

The Dignity of Man
Select Sermons

ISBN/EAN: 9783337160562

Printed in Europe, USA, Canada, Australia, Japan

Cover: Foto ©Lupo / pixelio.de

More available books at **www.hansebooks.com**

The Dignity of Man

SELECT SERMONS

BY

SAMUEL SMITH HARRIS, D.D., LL.D.

LATE BISHOP OF MICHIGAN

With a Memorial Address

BY

RT. REV. HENRY C. POTTER, D.D., LL.D.

BISHOP OF NEW YORK

CHICAGO
A. C. McCLURG AND COMPANY
1889

COPYRIGHT
BY SALLIE P. HARRIS
A.D. 1889

TO THE READER.

At the request of many friends I have prepared for publication this volume of my father's sermons. As its preparation has been a solace to me, I hope it may prove a consolation to those who have so sincerely mourned for him. To my father's friends, Bishop Henry C. Potter and Rev. Dr. Fulton, of New York, Gen. A. C. McClurg, of Chicago, Hon. James V. Campbell, Rev. Dr. McCarroll, Mr. Sidney D. Miller, and Mr. John H. Bissell, of Detroit, I am deeply indebted for their untiring interest and assistance.

SALLIE P. HARRIS.

Detroit, *February*, 1889.

CONTENTS.

	PAGE

INTRODUCTION. BY THE HONORABLE JAMES V. CAMPBELL, LL.D. 13

MEMORIAL ADDRESS. SERMON BY THE RIGHT REVEREND HENRY C. POTTER, D.D., LL.D. 47

Sermon I.

SHEPHERDHOOD 79

    He that entereth in by the door is the shepherd of the sheep. — ST. JOHN x. 2.

Sermon II.

THE DIGNITY OF MAN 93

    And God said, Let us make man in our image, after our likeness: and let them have dominion over the fish of the sea, and over the fowl of the air, and over the cattle, and over all the earth, and over every creeping thing that creepeth upon the earth. So God created man in his own image, in the image of God created he him. — GEN. i. 26, 27.

Sermon III.

THE INDIGNITY OF SIN 108

    But he that sinneth against me wrongeth his own soul: all they that hate me love death. — PROV. viii. 36.

Sermon IV.

REDEMPTION 122

And thou shalt call his name Jesus : for he shall save his people from their sins. — ST. MATT. i. 21.

Sermon V.

ETERNAL LIFE 137

Verily, verily, I say unto you, He that heareth my word, and believeth on him that sent me, hath everlasting life, and shall not come into condemnation; but is passed from death into life — ST. JOHN v. 24.

Sermon VI.

THE SIGNS OF THE TIMES 151

The Pharisees also with the Sadducees came, and tempting desired him that he would show them a sign from heaven. He answered and said unto them, When it is evening, ye say, It will be fair weather: for the sky is red. And in the morning, It will be foul weather to-day: for the sky is red and lowering. O ye hypocrites, ye can discern the face of the sky; but can ye not discern the signs of the times? — ST. MATT. xvi. 1-3.

Sermon VII.

HOME 163

God setteth the solitary in families. — Ps. lxviii. 6.

Sermon VIII.

MY NEIGHBOR 175

If ye fulfil the royal law according to the scripture, Thou shalt love thy neighbor as thyself, ye do well: but if ye have respect to persons, ye commit sin, and are convinced of the law as transgressors. — ST. JAMES ii. 8, 9.

Sermon IX.

BUSINESS 189

And that ye study to be quiet, and to do your own business, and to work with your own hands, as we commanded you; that ye may walk honestly toward them that are without, and that ye may have lack of nothing. — 1 THESS. iv. 11, 12.

Sermon X.

REPENTANCE 201
    From that time Jesus began to preach, and to say, Repent: for the kingdom of heaven is at hand. — St. Matt. iv. 17.

Sermon XI.

SONS OF GOD 212
    But as many as received him, to them gave he power to become the Sons of God, even to them that believe on his name: which were born, not of blood, nor of the will of the flesh, nor of the will of man, but of God. — St. John i. 12, 13.

Sermon XII.

HOPE 222
    Beloved, now are ye the sons of God, and it doth not yet appear what we shall be: but we know that, when he shall appear, we shall be like him; for we shall see him as he is. And every man that hath this hope in him purifieth himself, even as he is pure. — 1 John iii. 2, 3.

Sermon XIII.

SELF-SACRIFICE 231
    Hereby perceive we the love of God, because he laid down his life for us: and we ought to lay down our lives for the brethren. — 1 John iii. 16.

Sermon XIV.

THE ONLY GOSPEL FOR THE POOR 243
    Jesus answered and said unto them, Go and show John again those things which ye do hear and see: the blind receive their sight, and the lame walk, the lepers are cleansed, and the deaf hear, the dead are raised up, and the poor have the gospel preached to them. — St. Matt. xi. 4, 5.

Sermon XV.

A CHRISTMAS MESSAGE 256
    In him was life; and the life was the light of men. — St. John i. 4.

Introduction.

BY THE HON. JAMES V. CAMPBELL, LL.D.

THE DIGNITY OF MAN.

Introduction.[1]

IT would be impossible, in the space allowed by an introduction, to prepare anything which could be properly called a biographical notice; but most readers like to know something about an author whose writings they are to read, and especially where he is a great teacher, to whose

---

[1] The appearance of this Introduction with Bishop Potter's Memorial Address may call for explanation. It was prepared by request, just after the funeral of Bishop Harris, in view of a possible immediate publication of the volume of sermons; but it seemed to the writer, as to others, that no one could introduce these sermons to the public so gracefully as an associate in the House of Bishops, whose relations with Bishop Harris were not only affectionate and intimate, but confidential. Bishop Potter, at once, on being asked, agreed to perform this friendly service, suggesting, nevertheless, that there would be an advantage in presenting clerical and lay views together. Soon afterward the Standing Committee of the Diocese of Michigan invited him to deliver the address at the proposed memorial service, which was held on the twenty-second day of November, 1888. The result was the Memorial Address published in this volume, which presents the character of Bishop Harris so truly and so tenderly that nothing more could be desired; but at the courteous proposal of Bishop Potter, who said he had purposely avoided covering the same ground, this Introduction is retained. — J. V. C.

teachings they are invited to listen. To furnish some such information, it is not necessary at this time to trace the life of Bishop Harris back to childhood or even to early manhood. His life was eventful; but rather for its varying phases than for any personal adventures or strange incidents. He was a soldier, a lawyer, and a clergyman, before he ceased to be a young man, and he was but in middle age when his career ended. In each of his life periods he was a man of note, and his earlier experiences made their mark upon his character, while they broadened and strengthened his mental faculties. His work as a bishop was made easier, as well as more effective, by his training in different methods and his experience in varied affairs; but his new life had so far assimilated the elements of what preceded it, that it became a complete and harmonious whole, — a ripened product, and not a compound of various ingredients. It is therefore safe, and more convenient for the purposes of this volume, to begin any sketch of his career with his latest development, which is the one that produced all the work that will remain as his monument, and — what is much more important — shaped that strong and symmetrical personality which made the truest greatness of the noble man who so impressed himself on all who knew him.

After an early and somewhat precocious literary graduation, and an admission to the bar by special legislation because of his legal minority, Bishop Harris followed what to a young man of spirit, surrounded as he was, became inevitable, and was a soldier in the Southern Army. He served through the war honorably, and gained a reputation for humanity and magnanimity as well as bravery. His subsequent career at the bar was almost phenomenal in its rapid success. He was eloquent, laborious, and mature and wise beyond his years, and had already reached a large practice and a large income when he gave up the certainty of professional eminence and entered the ministry, which offered no inducements but an opportunity for self-sacrifice and devotion.

But when he began to minister to congregations, he at once became known as one who had an important work laid upon him. He labored for some years in the South, and became rector of the principal church in New Orleans, where he remained till he went to Chicago. His last charge was St. James's Church in Chicago. It was a parish of strong and energetic men, able to appreciate his intellect and his character; but it had suffered as other interests had suffered, not many years before, in the terrible fire that laid that city desolate. The brave rector became the worthy and beloved head of a brave band of Christian workers, and in due time the church more than regained its old prosperity. Quietly, without pretension, he accepted the various representative places which seemed to come to him by natural succession, and in the General Convention he became an active member and a forcible and respected debater, and accepted and performed important business duties with efficiency. He was offered and declined one of the bishoprics of his adopted State, because his people at that time needed him, and he would not desert them. During the yellow-fever epidemic at the South in 1878 his activity in getting aid for the sufferers gained him the same general regard, without reference to race or creed, which he won elsewhere during all his ministry.

In 1879 the Diocese of Michigan, at its Annual Convention in June, was under the necessity of choosing a bishop. After some failures to agree upon candidates presented to the laity for concurrence, Dr. Harris was nominated by the clergy for confirmation. The convention contained the most able lay representation ever known in that body; and yet his career had been so modest that while there was nothing suggested against him, there was very little known of him. He was chosen by no more than the requisite majority. But as soon as the news of the choice reached abroad, the telegraph brought in a few hours such numerous and convincing congratulations, that had there been time to consult the senders before the vote was taken, the lay vote would probably have been substantially solid in his favor.

His consecration took place Sept. 17, 1879, three days after he had completed his thirty-eighth year. The necessity of having it at such a time in the week as would not interfere with the engagements of the clergy in their parishes made it impossible to appoint it, as would have been desirable, on his birthday. It was also the strong wish of his people in Chicago to have him set apart to his high office in his own church; but there were prevailing reasons for having the consecration in Michigan. It was held in St. Paul's Church, Detroit, the oldest in the city and State, which was organized in 1824, when there was no other Episcopal church between Lake Erie and the Pacific Ocean; and when Michigan Territory, with a white population less than that of most small cities, included within its jurisdiction all of the country in the same latitude with the Rocky Mountains.

The occasion brought together an unusual number of bishops, and personal friends of the new bishop from remote parts of the Union. The consecrating bishop was Richard Hooker Wilmer, of Alabama, — the State where he was born, — who had introduced him into the ministry, and who loved him as a son. When the great congregation saw the solemn but hearty gladness with which the eminent prelates welcomed their new associate, and when they looked on him, as his majestic form and noble countenance impressed every one with the conviction that he was an unmistakable and honest leader of men, they thanked God and took courage. They were not disappointed.

Bishop Harris at once took measures to inform himself of the state of affairs in his diocese. His quick apprehension and systematic habits made that an easy task, as far as it could be performed without personal visitation in each parish, which came speedily. His first sermon was preached in St. Paul's Church, Detroit, at the earliest opportunity, and it gave a clear idea of his conception of a bishop's functions. It is the first sermon in this volume. As the season was advancing, and the Upper Peninsula was not accessible readily in cold weather, he made his first visitation in that part of the State, and impressed every one as favorably with his wisdom and capacity for business as he had with his personal merits.

On one of these occasions, being pressed for time, and likely to be detained at Detour, at the mouth of St. Mary's River, he procured an open Mackinaw boat manned by two lads, and crossed over the open water forty miles to Cheboygan, in weather by no means serene, and had to put his own hands to the oars to carry the boat to port. He continued to visit the parishes until he had seen all of them. In all cases he had conferences with vestries as well as ministers, and he stirred up the church spirit wherever he went. He had the valuable and somewhat rare faculty of remembering names and faces, and he seldom had any difficulty in recalling persons he had met, and under what circumstances he met them. He had thus in his mind, for ready reference, a sufficient knowledge of the situation and peculiarities of all the parishes.

But, busy as he was with his diocesan affairs, he had already begun to look beyond them to their more indirect bearings. As was more fully exemplified in his subsequent writings and addresses, he had an intense devotion to the civil institutions of the United States, and believed it a necessary part of his religious duty to fulfil the obligations of a citizen. As this view, often and strongly expressed, did not always commend itself to some scrupulous souls who do not seem to regard the precept for rendering his own to Cæsar as one of perpetual obligation, it is worthy of a moment's attention. The published course of "Bohlen Lectures" delivered by him some years later contains a series of illustrations of his general theory. He believed all the essential organizations of human society as no less a part of the Divine scheme for human civilization than the religious system ordained by the Ruler of the Universe. From the family to the State, as to the Church, he held that society was one of the appointed instruments for the preservation and advancement of humanity. He believed, further, that the plans of the Almighty are ordered generally by law, rather than by special interferences, and that nations were usually left to form their own institutions, subject to the responsibility for their conduct, which history has so abundantly exemplified. He believed that a popular government, such as is provided for and regulated by American Constitutional principles, is the best of all forms, and better fitted than any other, if rightly maintained and administered, to secure to each citizen his complete equality before the law, and his freedom and prosperity. And believing this, he was as firmly convinced that so much of church polity as is of human cognizance should be framed as closely as possible in analogy to the scheme of secular affairs, keeping civil and religious freedom in harmonious relations, and regarding both as an inheritance from the Lord. His intense patriotism and his pride as an American citizen were in his sight a plain and religious duty. Accordingly he desired to make prominent in his teachings not only the religious character of the duty to respect the rights of our neighbors, but to respect and cherish the fabric of human society as the divinely ordered means for protecting those rights, which have never been respected and cannot be protected without law and government.

Convinced as he was that there could be no safe union of Church and State, he was convinced also of the necessity for placing religion prominently before the world as the best means of quickening men in the performance of all duties, and impressing them with the value and universal efficacy of pure motives as springs of action. And as the period of education is the time when character is formed, he was solicitous to bring such forces to bear upon students as would help them to become good citizens, by making them recognize duty instead of policy as the guide of their lives.

The next day after his consecration he first expressed his solicitude concerning religious influences upon the students of the Michigan University. Admitting the impracticability of making theological teaching a part of the University course, it was evident that the ordinary parish

influences were inadequate to reach and control
large bodies of persons, who were usually men
grown, and masters of their own conduct, and
many of whom had no religious ties whatever.
He thought that Christian churches could not act
efficiently without some place to which students
could be attracted by legitimate attractions, and
furnished means of companionship and quiet rec-
reation, as well as facilities for religious cultivation
in subjects not within the scholastic or professional
courses. The idea was hailed with pleasure by the
University teachers and the people of Ann Arbor,
as well as of other parts of the State, who began
to look to him as the one capable of putting into
shape a purpose that in its crude form was so full
of promise. He had said to persons who were
the strongest supporters of the University, what
at first seemed paradoxical, — that he was more
deeply concerned in its welfare than they were.
Its truth was recognized when he pointed out that
a bishop is bound to his diocese for life, while
other men can at all times change their residence
and go where they please. The history of the
development of this idea would form a long but
instructive chapter by itself. He revolved it continually. Scheme after scheme was urged upon
him, and to some of them he was inclined strongly,
until convinced they would not do. He became

satisfied, some time before his plan finally became determined, that while any scheme adopted should be under his supervision, and kept in harmonious relations with the church which had called him to its service, its advantages should be open to all students, of whatever creed, who desired to profit by its facilities. During the latter days, when it was gradually acquiring symmetry, he was approached by several theological students of other denominations, who urged him earnestly to bring his work into operation. The patient waiting and reflection of several years at last brought him to a satisfactory conclusion. Without going into full details, it may be said that it includes a spacious building furnished with lecture and reading rooms, library, parlors, and rooms for physical exercises, under charge of a guild, made up chiefly of students and professors electing their own agencies, and left with a very large discretion in management, subject to the approval of the bishop. They were authorized to conduct general literary exercises, and procure ordinary lecturers, with the same approval. To provide the specially religious features of the plan, three or more annual courses of lectures were contemplated, each course to be reasonably endowed, and conducted by lecturers appointed by the bishop. These lectures are all designed to deal with those subjects especially which bear on the relations of religion with society and education; and these courses are open to all who choose to attend them. Single lectures are also contemplated, by persons appointed by the bishop, on similar topics. The Baldwin Lectureship has been fully endowed, and two courses delivered under it have already been published. Progress has been made with the others, and the experience thus far has been satisfactory, and is believed to have solved one of the most important problems of education. The Hobart Guild Hall is a successful venture.

This has been referred to at some length, because it is the only instance in which the purposes and ideas of Bishop Harris, beyond his official work, have been materialized and made operative under his own care.

His first official efforts were made to extend the preaching of the gospel. In this work his energy and good judgment were both so apparent, that the contributions for Diocesan Missions were increased rapidly, and to an unhoped-for extent, and the increase has been progressive. Mission work has been enlarged and systematized, and many promising fields have been opened. Not very long after this impulse was received, one of those devastating fires occurred in the eastern part of the State which have become so dreaded in the timber districts, and a large section was laid waste, with complete destruction of farms and buildings, and some loss of life. Bishop Harris organized an active corps of assistants, and collected and distributed large contributions among the sufferers. Beyond this he obtained means for building comfortable places for worship, which became mission centres. His character and ways had acquired such admiration and confidence, that an attempt made to enable the parishes to gain enlarged power to contribute to missions, by relieving them from supporting the Episcopate, led to the collection in cash means, within a few weeks, of an addition to the Episcopal Fund of $50,000, all of which was due to faith in the bishop. Several thousand dollars of this came from personal admiration of his nobility and beauty of character, outside of church membership or attachment.

The story of his episcopate within his diocese becomes one of those fortunate narratives which have little to tell beyond steadily increasing peace and prosperity. The people are said to be happy who have no history; but that condition is only reached by the heroic and constant sacrifices of those who give themselves and their lives to secure its preservation. When any jar comes, it is found that the smooth motion was the result of great forces kept working under orderly restraint. The greatest peace is the work of the greatest energy and wisdom.

A bishop who achieves this, and only this, is justly reckoned as a faithful and wise steward, and his name is held in honor. Bishop Harris did all for his diocese that wisdom could suggest and fidelity and zeal accomplish. He never neglected his home duties for other occupations. The prosperity of the churches was foremost and continually in his mind and heart. He carried his heavy official burden cheerfully, and answered all calls promptly. His clergy leaned on him for advice and comfort as children on a loving father. When he visited their parishes, his coming was looked for and welcomed by old and young of every station, for the gentle courtesy and loving frankness of his personal recognition. He never chilled any one, however unimportant, by condescension or formal urbanity. As a high-bred Christian gentleman, and a true American, he respected the dignity of our common manhood.

But he had clear ideas of a field of duty which was not theological in the ordinary sense of that word, although it took in his sight the form of Christian obligation. Regarding, as has been already hinted, the Church and all its instrumentalities as placed here in activity, not only for God's glory but for the highest benefit of the human race, and especially of that part of it where his own lot was cast, he naturally kept before him the end as well as the means. He could not do this without seeing that other instruments and methods than those of the church were doing much, and might do more, to advance the prosperity and further the highest interests of his fellows and their organizations. His quick sympathies and tenderness led him first of all to lament the variances which defeat so much good, and the cruelties which crush out so much courage and ruin so many hopes. And he found in our schemes of education much lamentable disregard of the more exalting functions, and much fragmentary teaching, that lacked organic union with the vital forces of truth and wisdom. With no sanguine notions of wonders that he might accomplish, and no assumption that he had a special mission, he seized the frequent opportunities offered him of making public addresses before public audiences, at college commencements, congresses and conventions, and other gatherings where sound words are not irrelevant, and advocated the things he believed in with such force and eloquence that his words were not wasted. He delivered on one occasion at least, in the Michigan University, the annual Commencement Day Address, which has there superseded all the former ceremonies, and is intended to be a worthy ending to the scholar's course of training. His love for young men, and his enthusiasm for all that exalts and embellishes scholarship, and lifts it to the highest plane of dignity and usefulness, aroused him to exert all his powers to make his contribution worthy. His bright and piercing eyes, his sweet and powerful voice, his commanding stature and elegant grace of posture and gesture, and the kindly expression that made his handsome face radiant, charmed his entire audience, and they became responsive to him as a musical instrument to its master. His occasional visits and deliverances to students are among their best traditions. He presided at the Church Congress held in Detroit a few years ago, and not only made an opening address, which was not surpassed if it was equalled by any of the papers or speeches presented by the distinguished men who took part in the Congress, but attracted still more admiration by his course as a presiding officer. With firmness that allowed no dispute, and courtesy that made the discipline pleasant, he gave each topic its proper place and each speaker his allotted time, and no more, so that the programme was filled precisely as intended, and what is sometimes a rather chaotic assemblage was made a model of order.

While no one appreciated better the importance of the duties to which he had sacrificed his worldly prospects, and he had decided convictions that his religious associations were most accordant with primitive Christian polity, he felt a warm regard for, and was in hearty sympathy with, the sincere devotion of Christian ministers of other denominations in their religious labors. They were in his sight brethren serving the same Master, and doing his work. He gave, and they desired, no renunciation of convictions; but while their public services were distinct, they took sweet counsel together, and he was to many of them a father as well as a brother. They hastened to join in the honors rendered to his memory, and in pulpit and press, as in private conversation, they lamented for him as a great captain of the Lord's host, and a holy and humble man of God. One of the most powerful addresses he ever made was at the meeting of the Evangelical Alliance in Washington, not very long ago, which attracted attention everywhere, and has been referred to by the press since his death as placing him at the very front as a great orator and a great and large-minded man.

But his heart was especially interested in the

vital social problems which are exercising most thinking persons, and the solution of which is one of the pressing needs of our time. He held none of those Utopian ideas which look to the destruction of private interests and possessions, and he did not imagine that society would be set at rest by any levelling of fortunes at the expense of diligence and industry. He did believe that human society is largely at fault for the oppression that is done under the sun, and the power for mischief that is possible under laws and usages which facilitate irresistible combinations of men or of money to paralyze opposition. For this he set forth no panacea. He was too conscientious to champion any plan until it satisfied his sober judgment, after long study and reflection. But it was one of his cherished desires to make this his principal subject of consideration in the future, and in patience and perseverance to devise or aid others in devising means to diminish the evil and cultivate harmony. But of one thing he persuaded himself, and it is the theme of many utterances, — that the peace and good-will which were sung by the angels at the Nativity were the only absolute remedy. When times are out of joint, tempers become unreasonable; but every one knows that poverty is not half so bitter as lack of sympathy, and that there is no greater cruelty than wounding self-respect. This was the meaning of his uniform assertion of equality in rights under Divine and human law, which renders all honest work respectable, and denies the right of any one who buys another's service to assert that manhood is to be thrown into the bargain.

As Bishop Harris never used the pulpit for any purpose beyond that of preaching the gospel, there were many phases of life and action on which he could only address the public through the press or by secular addresses. He had not been long in his diocese before his genius and eloquence made him desired as a public speaker in various parts of the United States. While he never left home unless he could do so without prejudice to his home duties, his systematic order gave him many such opportunities, and he became popular and influential as an orator and moral teacher. Audiences loved to listen to him, and went home delighted as well as edified.

He gave some lectures in the New York Theological Seminary, in the special course at Kenyon College, at Philadelphia under the Bohlen endowment, and at several conventions of scholars and persons interested in reform and philanthropic work. Many of these were published in a fugitive form. The only book he ever published was the "Bohlen Lectures." These are a connected series, chiefly devoted to exemplifying the co-ordinate functions of religious and social order. They are thoughtful and suggestive, and full of practical wisdom. Their conciseness and logical arrangement render them attractive reading to intelligent and scholarly readers. It may be that dilution and expansion would have made them easier of digestion by some classes of readers; but their compact force and completeness indicate a master's work.

Bishop Harris generally spoke without referring to his notes. He committed so readily that he could always reproduce in speaking precisely what he had written. But he was an easy offhand speaker, and his speeches were as polished and complete in the one case as in the other. He had, however, such a conscientious desire to say nothing unguardedly, that it has been found, by reference to his papers, that on all occasions, social as well as public, he was in the habit of thinking out and writing down, when time permitted, what would be an appropriate utterance. It is not likely that when he rose to his feet he always or generally repeated what he had written with verbal fidelity. There are frequently occasions where a speaker who is preceded by others would find himself covering the same ground if he adhered to his previously written manuscript. No one ever knew him to fall into that difficulty. It is more likely that he wrote to fill his mind with the subject rather than the words. His manuscripts are generally if not always in his own handwriting. He was not inclined to use an amanuensis, but wrote very rapidly, and his pen moved with the thoughts.

When he had his mind intent on any subject upon which he wished to write, he not only studied and compared what he could find in books and other receptacles, but he loved to converse on it, and exchange views with others, whom he usually taught much more than they taught him, but who could often from their own experience or observation correct or confirm his impressions, or bring new light upon the matter.

But he did not seek his friends chiefly to sharpen his intellect or inform his mind. His nature was eminently social, and there were few more pleasant experiences than to meet him in his hours of rest and relaxation and listen to his genial talk, and exchange those conversational thoughts and pleasantries that have their practical side in cheerful refreshment, which is the wise man's medicine. Although he had not much leisure for pursuits which did not have some bearing on his life work, he had nevertheless a broad comprehension of what would aid it. There are many weapons in the scholar's armory, and many exercises which strengthen his faculties. He liked, when he could, to go back to the wisdom of the ancients, knowing that modern thoughts have sometimes been damaged in the borrowing. Plato was his chief favorite in ancient literature, and there was at least one side of his mind which would have made him congenial to the old philosopher. He had also paid much attention to the theories and discussions on ethnology and language; but while his mind was receptive, he did not surrender his judgment unconditionally.

While it is evident, from his various writings, and his private conversations, that he had his thoughts fixed intently in one direction, yet the subject was so many sided, and the scheme so large, that he never became a man of one idea, or a harper on one string. The harmonies of the universe are all in unison, but no mind is large enough to include all of them.

Soon after the bishop came to Michigan, an estimable lady of St. Paul's Church secured a lot on the island of Mackinac as a gift from Mr. Gurdon Hubbard of Chicago, conditioned on its improvement. She procured sufficient means to build a neat cottage and furnish it appropriately for summer use. The bishop and his family made it their summer refuge, where he found leisure for such work as he cared to do and needed quiet for doing, but where he spent much time in open-air enjoyments, and in social intercourse with congenial friends and neighbors. The house was far enough away from the summer bustle of the village and the crowd of the hotels to have all the merits of seclusion, while within a short distance was a colony of agreeable families to whom the cottage in the wood was as attractive as a field of clover to the bees.

This is an imperfect sketch of the way in which Bishop Harris's life and work were made manifest. His plan was one which counted all interests as subject to one family under the Divine scheme, however separately grouped or subdivided. And while in so short a life as his this could only be partly outlined, yet the adherence to this principle as the cardinal rule of harmonizing God's plans was itself a proof of the greatness of mind and character that made him a characteristic product and leading spirit of our time.

Yet, after all, true greatness is not in what is written or what is done, so much as in the man himself. The men who stand forth before others in the long procession of history have left very little of their works that we can look at and appreciate. But we know them, nevertheless, as heroes and benefactors, and we know that their goodly presence and the sound of their voice inspired love and confidence. When a truly great man appears, his greatness needs no expounding, and virtue emanates from his presence.

Bishop Harris, with all his intellectual power, his imposing appearance, his simple and moving eloquence, his executive ability, and the other qualities so often dwelt upon, may not in any one or all of these things have been beyond other men who never stood pre-eminent. And it is as difficult to analyze the more subtle elements which gave his personality its power and charm, as to apply scientific tests to the beauty of flowers or the glory of sunset. The finer qualities which excite love and trust as well as reverence and admiration elude description. In saying they exist, all is said that can be. But with this difficulty it would do the bishop's memory great injustice if some of these manifestations were not pointed out.

His patience and gentleness were not the result of indolent good-nature. Any one who knew him well discovered that the real secret of his uniform calmness was the absolute self-control which makes him that ruleth his spirit greater than he that taketh a city. His feelings were deep and tender, and had never lost their bloom. He was naturally and always sensitive. His observation was quick and his reading of character instinctive. His mind was not only logical, but very acute and discriminating, and he had a taste for metaphysical pursuits which, if he had been a secluded student and not a man of action, would probably have led him as safely as any solitary mind can go safely, yet with many perils, through all the labyrinths and mazes which find no end. But this capacity of fine discrimination, kept corrected by the test of daily experience of life and its facts, was of value to him, and enabled him to detect sophistry, and look at all the sides of each plan or question which he had to consider. His great love of intellectual diversions was one of the things in which self-denial was hardest and self-control most bracing. He had also not only a keen enjoyment of humor, but a love of poetry and of the finer products of literature which are so attractive to men of delicate sensibility. It may readily be imagined that he would have enjoyed shaping his own fancies in musical verse or as musical prose, which his fine ear would have guarded from discords, and his faultless taste would have made charming. If he indulged in such delights, he never made it known even to his friends. His style was chastened, in his sermons and essays, where he might have embellished it if he had chosen; and his memory was so full of accurately remembered gems of verse, that it is remarkable he did not glide off unconsciously into quotations or flights of fancy. He did indeed, but very seldom, adopt some poetical expression of an idea that would have lost force by other treatment, as he did in one instance incorporate into a sermon the beautiful reference in Wordsworth to the soul's premonitions of immortality. Some other equally happy uses of poetical extracts make us wish that his leisure and his sense of duty might have allowed him more indulgence. In his multiplied capacities he had the elements of a poet, which he discarded, and of an essayist, which he displayed to advantage in many ways, but never allowed to do holiday work. This man of refinement and elegant taste and culture, frank as a boy and magnanimous in thought and action, when thrown among the varied realities of life, where he was liable at all times to have his tastes and sensibilities and temper tried severely, acquired such admirable control of himself that his temper seemed never to be ruffled; he never indulged in sarcasm or even mild satire, and accepted cheerfully all the privations of comfort and elegance which came to him.

The office of a faithful bishop has its rewards, but it has also its great and small martyrdoms. He is condemned to a great deal of that worst kind of solitude, where absence of congenial spirits is aggravated by the importunity of vexatious ones. In a large diocese, the number of clergy and laymen who visit him, not on errands of social enjoyment, but to lay their burdens on him, as well as perhaps in some cases to add some weight to his own, is very considerable. Pious men of all kinds represent, very much as others do, many phases of human nature. Grace and fundamental goodness do not entirely obliterate the old Adam. A narrow mind sees nothing but folly in the broad wisdom of a great one. An obstinate disposition perseveres in stolid opposition, with small regard to reason. A vulpine nature, however sanctified, never moves in straight lines; bluntness may become insufferable impudence. Weak men shuffle off their own responsibilities on his broader shoulders, and then waste his time with getting up a pretence of activity.

A bishop may be made of stern enough material to bring them all to their bearings, and deal with them sharply and in plain language, and exhibit them to themselves as they appear to him. The world would not much blame him for doing so; but it would bring sullenness and vindictiveness or heartbreak. Bishop Harris received all men patiently and kindly, and, as far as human nature would respond to him, affectionately. If he could

not satisfy the unreasonable, or acquiesce in what
was wrong, he sent no one away wounded or
humiliated. And if some self-tormenting, over-
scrupulous person came to him morbidly invit-
ing penance and discipline, he encouraged him
to more manly and wholesome ways, and sent
him out rejoicing into the sunshine. The household is happy where the father's face is cheering
and comforting.

A life so devoted and beneficent is not always
a joyful one. But Bishop Harris was not only
cheerful and contented, but happy. He had one
great privation in the difficulty of always finding
congenial associates to discuss face to face the
subjects which interested him. But such enjoyment was not by any means so rare as to be
notable. He frequented, when he had leisure, a
club of intellectual men, who discussed all manner
of subjects freely and unceremoniously, and if they
did not help him in dealing with his special topics,
they sharpened his faculties, and gave him recre-
ation as well as profit. And it has happened to
him, as often happens to bright men of his kind,
that persons of entirely different genius and temperament became attached to him, and admired
him almost passionately.

To those whom he honored with his friendship
and attachment he was a charming companion,

full of brightness and animation, and confiding, tender, and sympathizing. He had a healthy taste for innocent enjoyments, and when he was worn down by confinement and worry, it delighted him to accompany a brother of the angle to the secluded waters of some solitary inlet on Lake Superior, or launch out from the coast, where his skill or good fortune generally gained him the larger share of the prey. He had a love of Nature in all its manifestations, and was a close observer of animals and plants; and animals loved him. One of the pleasures he had planned for himself, after he should return from his last journey, was a study of the ornithology of Michigan, with which he was anxious to become familiar.

His home-life, which was beautiful, will not be dwelt on here.

But some one who believes that a biographer should be inflexible as Rhadamanthus may ask, Was this man perfect? Good reader, this is not a biography, but the poor attempt of a friend who loved him to depict a part of his merits. In this forum there is no need of a Devil's Advocate to invent objections to canonization. What defects he had were not such as a friend need search out; and his enemies, if he had any, did not venture to trumpet them.

The fact that he grew greater and wiser continually, showed that he had once been behind his later growth. Happy is the man who, when he progresses, goes upward and not downward. He was pure, brave, tender, honest, faithful. He loved God and loved men. The faults or defects of such a character need not exercise the charity of any one.

In June last he went with his daughter and some friends to attend the Convention of Bishops of the British and American and Colonial Episcopal Churches, and to spend some time in travelling through Great Britain and the Continent, meaning subsequently to go to Greece, Egypt, and Palestine. He had become very much wearied by his labors at home before he went, and he devoted himself in England to the business of the Conference, and was obliged to undergo many of the more trying social ordeals, and gained no rest. On the 15th of July, while preaching in Winchester one of the sermons in this volume, he had a slight attack of vertigo, which for a moment disturbed him, but did not prevent him from completing his discourse. But within a day or two he began to grow weaker, and showed some signs of a lesion of the brain, and grew gradually more feeble, until at last he became unconscious, and on August 21, at sunset, he died. His funeral was celebrated solemnly in Westminster Abbey, and his memory was publicly and sincerely honored by Englishmen of mark and by his own countrymen. A sad company came with his mortal part across the Atlantic, and after a service in Grace Church, New York, his body was brought to Detroit, and his funeral rites were celebrated in St. Paul's Church. The streets were filled with mourning thousands who could not find room in the building, but remained in perfect order and quiet outside. His coffin rested on the spot where nearly nine years before he stood up and recited the vows which pledged him to the work of the Episcopate. He was laid in Woodmere, beside the grave of his little son, who had gone before, and welcomed him to Paradise.

JAMES V. CAMPBELL.

Memorial Address.

BY THE RT. REV. HENRY C. POTTER, LL.D.

SERMON

MEMORIAL OF THE RT. REV. SAMUEL S. HARRIS, D.D., LL.D., PREACHED BY THE BISHOP OF NEW YORK, AT THE DIOCESAN MEMORIAL SERVICE HELD IN ST. JOHN'S CHURCH, DETROIT, THURSDAY, NOV. 22, 1888.

And there was not among the children of Israel a goodlier person than he: from his shoulders and upward he was higher than any of the people.— 1 SAMUEL ix. 2.

THIS occasion is not biographical nor eulogistic, but memorial. Suffer me to emphasize the distinction, for it implicitly defines my task.

I should be glad if an extensive review of the life of our friend might hereafter be made, for it would be a work of enduring value; but this is not the place for it. As little is it the place for mere panegyric or eulogium. If the purpose of this holy house did not prohibit these, there is another restriction from which I should be unable to shake myself free. I am to speak this evening of one whom I greatly loved and deeply venerated, and I cannot forget that from the language of mere eulogy he would have recoiled with instinctive and resolute disapproval.

But he would hardly chide me, I venture to believe, if he knew that, in obedience to the voice of his stricken diocese, I had come here to-night to tell you what I remember of him, — to recall how in him, as I profoundly believe, the grace of God wrought with singular power and efficacy, and how in his natural characteristics, enriched and ennobled by the indwelling power of the Holy Ghost, there shone forth a Christian manhood at once strong and wise, and so worthy of our grateful imitation.

It is not, on the whole, an evil generation in which you and I are living; but there are, nevertheless, tremendous forces of evil which are at work in it. They threaten, some of us think, as never before, much that is sacred and venerable. They deny, with increasing frequency and audacity, the presence in the world of the supernatural. They deny the being of God and the operations of his Spirit. They disown his Word written and his Kingdom mystical, and for all these they demand, with more and more strenuous insistance, the evidence.

Well, we have come here to-night, men and brethren, to furnish the doubters of fundamental verities with that which, of all other kinds of evidence in such a question, is at once the most substantial and the most intelligible. We offer them the life and work of one who dwelt here among you, who went in and out among these homes and shops and offices, whom you knew, not merely in official ministrations but in the most intimate personal contacts (for of almost all men whom I have ever known he was the most approachable and accessible), and we ask you to explain such a man and such a life upon any other theory than its being consciously lived under a Divine inspiration and unreservedly consecrated to a Divine service. This thought will dominate my task this evening, and at once define and limit the words which I shall say to you. Forgive me if in any wise they shall seem to take on a tone of reminiscence too personal and individual. Others will bear, as others have borne, their testimony to this noble life. I can do little more than tell what I know from personal intercourse, irregular, alas! and often for long periods intermitted.

I first came to know Bishop Harris when, in the year 1880, he entered the House of Bishops for the first time, and took his seat as a member of that body. He had been consecrated on the 17th of September in the preceding year (1879), and the General Convention of our Church, which sat in 1880 in the city of New York, was the first occasion of his meeting his brethren in the Episcopate. He became a member of the House of Bishops about the same time that the late Bishop of Western Texas (Dr. Elliott), and the present Bishops of Kentucky (Dr. Dudley), West Virginia (Dr. Peterkin), and Louisiana (Dr. Gallcher) were chosen and consecrated; and when, as Secretary of the House of Bishops, I designated the seats of the prelates, who as Junior Bishops were placed adjacent to one another, I said, in playful allusion to the fact that each one of them had during our late Civil War been an officer in the Confederate service, " Gentlemen, I am afraid I shall have to nail up the United States flag on this part of the house," I remember, as though it were but yesterday, the kindly smile that broke over the face of the Bishop of Michigan, — a smile that not only showed to me that my friendly pleasantry had not been misinterpreted, but as it were opened a hitherto closed shutter in a house flooded inwardly with light and warmth. From that moment, I think, we understood each other, as it has ever since seemed to me, intimately; and the bond of brotherly regard and mutual confidence which then sprang into being grew and strengthened, until now, blessed be God! it reaches within the veil.

What a rich and gracious life it was which then disclosed itself! Samuel Smith Harris was, indeed, a Southerner in all that is best and most affluent in the name, and in nothing was this more singularly evident than in his early development and maturity. He was the son of an Alabama planter, Buckner Harris, Esq., of Autauga County, and his school-days began at the age of four years. One who was his teacher then[1] has communicated since his death to one of his children her recollection of those days; and these reminiscences are so simply and touchingly told that I cannot refrain from rehearsing them here. Says the writer: —

"Incidents do not make the chief impression upon my mind and heart, but rather the brilliant intellect which drew hard upon my own superior years and acquirements, the harmony and beauty of his character, and the royal graces of soul which magnetized admiration into love and loyalty. Among varied recollections clustering about a happy experience as teacher at the South, none have been more cherished by me than the associations with the school at Bushy Knob, Autauga County, Ala.

"Its situation was unique, placed, as the old school-house was, amid luxuriant vegetation, quite near the fordable and peaceful little stream, which on occasion became a rushing flood. Teacher and pupils were the only frequenters of this isolated spot, except on Sundays,

[1] Miss H. M. Perry.

when the adjacent church was transformed from its ordinary barn-like appearance into a sanctuary filled with devoutly earnest worshippers after the Hard-Shell Baptist pattern. You may have heard your dear father speak of the quiet retirement of this place. It was a retreat favorable to intimate intercourse between instructors and pupils, since even the long noon recess gave too brief time to take dinner at the widely scattered houses; but dinner-baskets furnished an abundant luncheon, brought sometimes by their own hands, sometimes sent by the hands of some not immortal Topsy. It was in these noonings that I especially learned to admire and love the character of 'little Sam Harris.' Why he was called ' little ' by his fellow-students was an unsolved problem, since he was tall for a boy between the years of ten and eleven, though quite slight in figure and of delicate appearance. He was a remarkably handsome boy to look upon, and of such attractive manners as to create the wish that he were more diminutive and were possessed of less dignity, so that one might indulge in the caressing demonstrations which sometimes fall to the lot of small boys of the same age; but we each took our luncheon into different corners of the room, and settling ourselves on the hard wooden benches, entered upon the intellectual intercourse afforded us during the delightful hour of leisure. It was not books that occupied us then, but talk. My enthusiasm for imparting knowledge was still in its youthful freshness, and he was an ardent, inquiring learner; and although it would be superfluous to recall the topics which supplied matter on these occasions, yet memory vividly presents to me the fact that I enjoyed intensely those days of which he writes to me in a letter in May, 1885, just after his return from a visit to the scenes of his boyhood: 'All the old days passed before me in a clear-drawn solemn vision, and none were more vivid or more joyous in memory than those which I passed under your kind and inspiring tuition. Indeed, I have never forgotten you, and have always thought of you with gratitude and affection.'

"It may be permitted to me to say just here that I aspire to no loftier praise, and crave no sweeter message of regard and remembrance, than is conveyed in these words.

"I think he pursued his studies not so much from ambitious desires as from strong love of knowledge, though ambition, too, was undoubtedly excited by friction with more mature minds. Though surpassing his companions in every study, he aroused no jealousy in them. He seemed to be made on a different plan and after a different pattern from themselves, and that apparently increased the warmth of their regard, and caused them to become gentle under the influence of his graciousness. I recall one particular time when one of the boys, called 'long Tom Smith,' rallied him on staying indoors, and a little scuffle ensued in trying to force him out. Sam came off victor, although his antagonist was large and strong enough to carry him out bodily. However, he was not generally averse to sports, but was an active, joyous, merry-hearted boy, whose companionship was desired and sought by the whole school, only at these noonings he indulged his preference for the society of his instructors. Those of his fellow-students at that time who may be living near the old haunts will, I am certain, heartily concur with me in rendering even more enthusiastic praise than I have ventured to indulge in. I shrink from expressing all the praise which affection suggests, lest a wound be given to the humility which prompted him to write, 'I do most sincerely trust that we may meet again in this world; but if that happiness should be denied me here, I do not doubt, if I shall be faithful, that we shall meet in the land of the living.' He was faithful to the end. It remains for me to follow his example."

From school Samuel Harris passed, at the age of fifteen, to the University of Alabama, which he entered in the year 1856. This was an early matriculation, but it would have occurred two years earlier still, had it not been for his extreme youth, on account of which he was refused admission. As it was, he entered sophomore, and was graduated three years later. His college life, a friend writes, was a very happy one, and he spent a large part of it in the exceptionally fine college library, which was afterward destroyed by fire. It was during his undergraduate life that he rendered to a friend whom he saved from drowning, and the scar of whose death-grip he bore upon his shoulders for years afterward, a service which became prophetic of his latest and highest calling.

From college, in the year 1859, he passed at once to the study of the law under Chancellor Keys, and was admitted to the bar in 1860, at the age of nineteen, a special act of the legislature authorizing his admission at that age. In the following year he married, and before the year had ended he was confronted with the problem of the Civil War, and entered the Confederate service.

It was said of Frederick W. Robertson, that if he had not been a clergyman he would have been a soldier; and he more than once implied himself that some of his strongest sympathies and enthusiasms were with that service. It was not so with the young lawyer from Autauga County. The life of the camp was not congenial to him, and with his refined instincts and sensitive nature we can well understand it. But he had a keen sense of honor and of duty, and these held him to his tasks, principally those of a staff officer, until the end. When that had come, he removed to New York and resumed the practice of the law, which he continued until the year 1868. This page of his life is interesting and characteristic. His practice, from choice, was mainly in the Supreme Court. He disliked and disdained the arts by which juries are too often influenced, and still more the sharp practice by which Justice is too often wounded in the house of her friends. But his pursuit of his profession was eminently successful, and he never lost a cause. Meanwhile, his love of letters continued to reassert itself. He wrote a novel, which was published in 1868, called "Sheltern," of which a discriminating friend says that, while open to criticism "as to style and technique, the plot is good, and shows quite decided powers of imagination. But," the same friend adds, "the chief fault of the book [of course he is speaking of it as a work of fiction] is that from end to end the writer moralizes like a born Scotchman. In fact, if I did not know who the writer was, I should have said that he was a *preacher*, or ought to become one."

Already, in other words, the spell of his great vocation was upon him. And so it is not surprising to find the venerable bishop, Dr. Richard H. Wilmer, of Alabama, whose place in this commemorative service I am unworthily filling, and whose absence from this pulpit you cannot regret as much as I do, writing of this period in the history of Bishop Harris in these words: —

"There are many old citizens of Autauga County, Ala., who dwell fondly upon the early days of Bishop Harris, and love to speak of that refinement and courtesy of manner which characterized him through life. The writer of these lines will speak of what he personally knows.

"I find upon my Episcopal Records the confirmation of Samuel S. Harris at St. John's, Montgomery, Jan. 17, 1866. At that time I had no personal acquaintance with him, and did not again meet him until some time in the autumn of 1867. I often recall the interesting circumstances connected with that meeting. I had been that day pondering the question, — when does not a bishop ponder it? — 'Where shall we find the right men to fill up the ranks of the ministry?'

"Riding out home in a street-car, my attention was drawn to a stranger seated in the car. So much was I impressed by his singularly refined and intelligent countenance, that I said to an acquaintance, 'That is the sort of man I am looking for.' 'Who is he?' said my friend. 'I do not know,' I replied; 'but there is something in that man.' His whole presence attracted me, and I indulged in speculation as to his future life, longing to put my hands upon him for the service of the King.

"The car at last reached my gate, and I got out. The stranger followed me, and immediately said, 'This is Bishop Wilmer, is it not?' I assented, and then he said, 'I am Harris, — Samuel Harris. I am come, Bishop, to offer myself to you for the ministry, if you will have me. I have been practising law in New York, but I feel called to another vocation, and I have my letter of transfer from the Bishop of New York (Horatio Potter), and wish to enter the ministry in my native State.'

"It may be imagined how we spent that night, and with what feelings of gratitude to God I marked out his studies and licensed him to act as lay-reader in St. John's, Montgomery, that church being then without pastoral care. The good people of St. John's will long remember his sojourn among them. When he was ordained deacon, shortly after, there was a general desire on the part of the congregation to elect him to the vacant rectorship; but I resisted it for the reason that I was unwilling to have him dwarfed by an amount of labor too great almost for one of maturer years and fuller preparation.

"February 10, 1869, I ordained him deacon in St. John's, Montgomery. He was presented for ordination by the Rev. J. F. Smith, a dear friend of his and of his father's house.

"June 30, 1869, I ordained him priest in the same church where he had received confirmation and deacon's orders.

"At that time he was called to the rectorship of the church at Columbus, Ga. His career since that time at Trinity, New Orleans, and at St. James, Chicago, is known to the Church.

"Again we met at his consecration to the Bishopric of Michigan. He said that I had confirmed him, ordained him deacon and priest, and that now his wish was that I should officiate as the consecrating bishop.

"The Standing Committee have now requested me to officiate at his memorial service. It seemed most fitting that I should perform for him this last service, but I did not feel equal to it. Accumulating labors and declining strength warned me that some other and younger man — some one who had been thrown into more intimate relations with him during his episcopal life, and had caught something of his inspiration — would discharge the duty more acceptably. If life be measured by its interest and intensity, he died full of years as of honors. Few men have compressed more of labor into a brief period. All that he had of natural attractiveness and gracious influences he consecrated to the Master. His Master was satisfied with the servant's work. Ere midday he had finished a full life's task. 'Even so, Father!'"

This is the brief outline of his life; and, as I began by saying, it is not the office of such an occasion as this even to attempt to fill it out. That is a task which demands a much larger opportunity, even as I hope it may find to perform it a far more competent hand.

But even as we review the outline there stand out, here and there, incidents which are at once characteristic and illustrative of the whole. Bishop Harris was pre-eminently a devout man, to whom the personal element in religion was before all else of consequence. And so it came to pass that in his earlier ministry his sympathies went out in directions where he thought he saw evidences of pre-eminent sancity, reverence, and consecration. But where, on nearer approach, he discovered the semblances of such things rather than the things themselves, no pride of consistency prevented him from correcting his previous impressions and modifying that course of action which they had determined. He was a Churchman from patient study, and profound conviction based upon that study. His law practice had been in the upper courts, and, as the friend from whom I have already quoted writes of him, just because "his study had been constitutional law and equity, and not the arbitrary rules of practice," and just because "constitutional law deals with historical facts and the historic development of institutions," therefore it was that when he came to the study of the Church he was ready to appreciate the divine principles of its historic life, and its development as an institution. To him the Church was the spiritual kingdom of God in the world; and hence to him every spiritual force and energy in the world is really of and belongs to the Church, and men may be in and of the Church without themselves knowing it, or even while vehemently denying it.

He did not disesteem his office as a priest of God, and neither did he belittle it. The Church he held to be a priestly body; and the priesthood of the laity is, he maintained, a cardinal fact which it is the pressing need of the time to realize, no less than that of the ministry. As to the ministry, he held, with increasing emphasis, that it must vindicate its claim to that title by ministering in all things; and one of the texts which he oftenest preached from was, "The Son of man came not to be ministered unto, but to minister." Of the Episcopate, he held that it is a function of the ministry, which is weakened and not strengthened by isolation from whatever is included in that larger term.

As he advanced in years, and in knowledge of

books, of men, and of his age, there is no doubt that the prophetic office grew to be of pre-eminent consequence in his judgment; and his estimate of it, and of its duty in our generation, is set forth with impressive force and clearness in the lectures which he delivered before the General Theological Seminary.

It was along this line that he aimed to work in his efforts for the reunion of Christendom. He believed profoundly with De Maistre, that our Anglican branch of the Church Catholic resembles one of those chemical intermediaries which bring into harmonious combination things that are repugnant to one another; and he held that as the Church of the Reconciliation we had a ministry of teaching to discharge with large and inexhaustible patience and love. For this work his own experience peculiarly trained him; for he had (rare and happy preparation for his ministry!) known the laity as one of them, first as a soldier and then as a lawyer, and he could see burning questions as bishops, priests, and deacons too often fail to do, from the layman's standpoint, as well as from his own.

Moreover, he had been through deep waters in his mental experience, and did not escape what has been called "the malady of our times." What he learned in those hours of darkness he never

forgot; and when he emerged from them with
their scars upon his grave and thoughtful countenance, he was better fitted than he had ever
been before to understand the meaning of his
priesthood, and the nature of his message and
ministry to his fellow-men. The tone of self-confident dogmatism, if it had ever been there,
had vanished. The childlike humility was deepened, the love of God and of his fellow-men was
enlarged, and that noble vision of the Church's
office in the world, which with such rare eloquence and splendid courage he set forth in his
address before the recent Conference in Washington, became to him a daily and ennobling
inspiration.

And thus swiftly he had ripened and greatened,
until men's eyes all over the land were turned to
him with ever-growing appreciation, interest, and
hope. "Among all the children of Israel there
was not a goodlier person than he: from his
shoulders and upward he was higher than any
of the people."

"From his shoulders upward." No one who
ever saw Bishop Harris could fail to be impressed
by his noble and stately presence. Physical qualities are not always, nor perhaps often, indications
of those that are higher, and greatness of stature
or bulk may very easily be accompanied by

meagreness of intellect and meanness of nature. But Saul was great, we read, "from his shoulders upward;" and I suppose the words may be taken to indicate a certain kingly quality in mien and bearing which indicated the royal gifts which animated the man. At any rate the words, when we think of Bishop Harris in connection with them, have a peculiar and pregnant significance. As the head crowns the body, and as so the noblest part of a man is "from his shoulders upward," so in him these qualities of which the home is the brain, and the head with its sensitive and expressive features is the fittest symbol, were the noblest and most regal of all.

1. But, first of all, let me not forget to say he had great qualities of heart. Able men are not always — not very often, I was tempted to say — lovable men, and the reason is not far to seek. But Bishop Harris was pre-eminently a lovable man; and that simply because his own nature was enriched by a strong spring of sympathy and tender regard for his fellows. No pride of intellect made him imperious, impatient, or contemptuous. He drew to him the hearts of children, of poor men and women, of those perplexed and in trouble, of the miserable and outcast, and made them captive by his own love for them, and by his ever helpful revelation of that love.

"He was the best friend I had in this world," said a prominent business man in Chicago, whose words, as they appeared in a journal of that city, I cannot refrain from quoting here: —

"There are many in this city to-day who at the turning-point of their commercial career, when everything looked black, ruin staring them in the face, have sought out the kindly pastor, and in the seclusion of his study found relief. The world has marvelled at the wonderful recuperative spirit Chicago business men have shown in times of commercial disaster. A different tale would be told if the walls of Dr. Harris's old study could recount what they have seen and heard. 'Be honorable, and among honest men you have nought to fear,' was his maxim.

"I remember one man who had been living in rather expensive style, but who, by a sudden turn in the wheat market, found himself on the verge of collapse. None of his friends had the least intimation of the state of affairs; but, as he afterward told me, Dr. Harris approached him one day, and in curious manner led up the conversation to a point where nothing short of a deliberate falsehood could help him to conceal his straits from his pastor.

"'I never could remember,' he said, in relating the circumstances, 'how it all came about. But we had been laughing and joking only a few minutes before, when I found myself opening up my inmost secrets to the doctor, and I have never ceased to thank God that I did so. He took pencil and paper, and when I had given him a statement of my terrible condition, he proceeded, like a skilful surgeon, to lay bare the wounds that were killing me, not sparing me one jot in matters that I had always expected to bury with myself; but before we had completed the investigation, he had shown me a way out of my difficulties, arduous enough it is true, but nevertheless a safe and sure one, as the sequel proved. I often spoke to him about the matter later, and was especially curious to know where he had obtained such a mastery of intricate business matters,—a point on which clergymen are usually the most ignorant. Said he, "True sympathy between pastor and people can never exist unless the former studies the evils which may afflict the latter, and *vice versa*. I find the people here sympathetic in my troubles and difficulties, and why should I not reciprocate the feeling?"'"

Why, indeed, one may well say, if only one has the gift to feel, and the rarer gift to give expression to that feeling!

Let me reproduce here one other incident illustrative of that nobility of the heart which I think you will agree with me was so pre-eminently characteristic of Bishop Harris. I take it from the same journal, and its homely and outdoor characteristics render it in no wise unworthy, it seems to me, of some more prominent record than it has already found: —

"We were walking along one of the streets of New Orleans," said a friend of the bishop, "when we met a big rough fellow who directly he caught sight of the bishop came to a sudden halt and seemed doubting whether to approach or not.

"'Well, John!' cried the bishop, extending his hand to the man. The fellow wiped his huge palm on his corduroy trousers before venturing to touch the proffered hand, and his bronzed features fairly beamed with pleasure at the bishop's recognition. Noticing the man's nervousness, I withdrew a few paces, as I knew of old that it was more than probable that the conversation would be one wherein an outsider would be *de trop*.

"Pretty soon the bishop rejoined me and told me that the man was a lumberman for whom he had done a trifling service in Upper Michigan. The nature of the trifling service I did not inquire, as I knew how apt the bishop was to minimize his own efforts.

"The next day I was out walking alone, when I met the Michigan man. Recognizing me as a friend of the bishop, he stopped to speak, and held out a brawny hand to me.

"'Ise mighty glad to see you, sir,' he said. 'I reckon you be a friend of the bishop.'

"'Yes, sir, I am proud to say I am.'

"'Proud? Well, I should think so. Ther ain't a man in the hull country what should n't be proud to shake hands with him.'

"'Do they think so much of him in Michigan as that?' I inquired.

"'As much as that? I tell you what it is,'— confidentially,—'ther boys has been talkin' among themselves, and they've about decided to make him Governor of Michigan.'"

The incident is homely, I have said, and some of you may think it scarcely congruous with the solemnities of this place and this occasion. But when one goes beneath the rough exterior of the incident, what a fine strong fibre of sympathy, of reality, of large-heartedness shines through it all! Bishop Harris never forgot his good-breeding, his refinement, his somewhat stately and (alas for the age in which it is so!) somewhat old-fashioned courtesy. But then, he never forgot his manhood, nor the manhood of his fellow-men. To put himself in touch with that, always to recognize and honor it, no matter what the garb it wore, — this was the characteristic of one whose warm and catholic kindliness of nature, whose breadth of vision and largeness of sympathy made the motto of Terence, "Humanus sum," and the rest, — "I am a man, and nothing human is alien to me," — his motto in all the manifold activities of his tireless life.

2. But again, these great qualities of the heart were dominated in Bishop Harris by qualities of the mind which were equally great. We may not forget, in recalling the rare man whom we are here this evening to remember, that his work was ended at a time when the best work of many men is just beginning. The years from twenty-five to forty-five are years of active service, it is true, in most lives, but they are no less years of the education and ripening of the best powers. And yet when these were ended with Bishop Harris, he had al-

ready accomplished tasks which, both as to character and quality, are, I venture to think, some of the most memorable in the intellectual history of our Church and our time. To some of them I have already alluded, and to others I can refer but briefly. But taking two only of them, they illustrate the highest quality of intellectual excellence, as it seems to me, in two very opposite directions. One of the things which Bishop Harris was permitted to accomplish of largest and most impressive significance was the founding, at the seat of the University of Michigan, of Hobart Hall and the Baldwin lectureship. The problem of Christian education is one of which the Church has attempted a solution in many ways, and nowhere with conspicuous success. She has scattered her energies, and, too often, missed her noblest opportunities.[1] Nothing, as I conceive, has indicated so unerringly the line of action along which these mistakes must be corrected, as the line which Bishop Harris thought out, and amid many difficulties so successfully built upon. It stamped him as one with a statesmanlike vision, and the rarest wisdom and discrimination in converting into a potential reality a really noble conception. It revealed the true office of the Church, and the true method and agency for best discharging that office. Undoubtedly, as some one has said of him,

[1] See page 75.

he was happy in a rare opportunity. Ah! yes. It is what the world says of those whom they are fond of calling "lucky men." But it is the men who, when the rare opportunity presents itself, have the wisdom to discern and the courage to seize and improve it, who have been its leaders and teachers and masters from the beginning, and that, verily, by divine right.

And so of another remarkable feature in the intellectual life of the late Bishop of Michigan, — I mean his "Bohlen Lectures on Christianity and Civil Society." I am at a loss to understand the strange failure of his contemporaries to recognize the rare qualities of this really great work, and I can only explain it by assuming that it must somehow have escaped the notice of thinking men. Nothing has been (so far as I saw them) more superficial, more utterly inadequate in almost every element of intelligent appreciation, than the reviews of this book which appeared when the first edition was published. A second has recently followed it, in allusion to which I observe that a religious journal lately remarked that upon the question at issue Bishop Harris had not spoken the last word. Possibly not; but, so far as I know, he has spoken the clearest, most discerning, and most conclusive word which has been spoken in our generation. I speak with what some of those who hear me may regard as undue confidence in this matter. Of course I speak only my own convictions. But having been led during the past year to read some forty volumes by different authors on the same general subject, I can only say that the one writer among them all who seemed first to have started out with a firm grasp of certain great principles and then to have followed them in a philosophic temper, so calm and serene as to make his pages an increasing delight, to their logical conclusions, and that with a reasoning at once lucid, vigorous, and irresistible, was the dear friend and teacher whom we are here to mourn to-night. I am no prophet nor the son of a prophet; but believe me when I tell you that the question which in those lectures to which I have referred your late bishop discussed, — the question of the relations to each other of the Church and the State, — is a question fraught, in our not very distant national future, with grave and portentous issues. And no less firmly am I persuaded that in the solution of that question and all the kindred questions of the relations of Christianity to human society, the great but imperfectly understood principles which Bishop Harris, with the hand of a master, so clearly and conclusively demonstrated, are the principles upon which those issues can alone be permanently and happily settled. To have rendered such a service to his age and the Church, — this is to have made them both, I think you will agree with me, his lasting debtors.

3. But greater than even intellectual excellence is moral excellence, — and rarer! And here, I think, our father and brother departed shone brightest of all. I do not know that he was singular in a clear perception of the right. Many men have that, though it is oftener than many of us think clouded by an apparent incapacity to appreciate nice moral distinctions; but in Bishop Harris a fine moral intuition had been ennobled and strengthened by scrupulous discipline and the highest inspiration. His conscience enlightened by the Holy Spirit, and not any wish, ambition, or appetite, was his master. With singular gentleness he united singular fearlessness; and if a thing appeared to him to be clearly his duty, that, with him, was enough. He was not impatient of counsel. It always seemed to me one of the best indications of his real greatness that he so often sought it; but when he had received it, he formed his own judgment in simple dependence upon God and in utter fearlessness as to the consequences. A friend,[1] to whose recollections of him I have already referred, has recalled an incident in the General Convention of 1874, to which

[1] Rev. Dr. John Fulton.

Dr. Harris (as he then was) was a deputy, which impressively illustrates this. It occurred in connection with a discussion in regard to the ritual law of the Church, which, he maintained, was to be found primarily in the prayer-book, and which therefore could not be constitutionally changed or modified by canon. The report of a committee on this subject, which took a different view, was adopted by the House of Deputies by an immense majority; but Dr. Harris voted against it with only five others, and these deputies who were supposed to be identified with what are known as most "extreme" views. He expected that his vote would cost him his parish, and said so; but that consideration did not cause him to hesitate or to swerve from what he regarded as the path of duty. It is an interesting and suggestive fact, which may here be incidentally noted, that the House of Bishops concurred in his position, and rejected the proposed canon.

Such an act was typical. If I were at liberty, I might match it with similar action which distinguished his course when, later, he came to have a seat in the House of Bishops; and you, I am sure, who knew and watched him in the rare openness and transparency of his daily walk and conversation as he went in and out among you, could confirm it by abundant testimonies which would be the result of your own long-continued observation. He was a power in this community, wherever men came to know him, because of his large sympathies, his strong intellect, but most of all by his unbending integrity. There is one relation in which, did time permit, I should rejoice to speak of him, — I mean his relation to his clergy, which, if I could tell its story here, would pre-eminently illustrate this. With what affectionate solicitude he concerned himself for their interests, watched for their welfare, sympathized with their burdens, counselled them in their perplexities and failures. Is not all this true? Yes; but is it not most of all true that in that paternal and judicial relation which he sustained to them he forever held up before them the standard of a high moral ideal, and in his own words and acts consistently translated righteous principles into righteous conduct? And this it was, more than all else, that, in all that he was and did, made him a power for God and for good.

It would violate the proprieties of this place if I were to speak of your bishop in those relations, most sacred and most tender, which he sustained to those nearest to him. But the Office for the Consecration of Bishops declares that a bishop must be one that "ruleth well his own house;" and the influence of such an example as his in every domestic relation will long live to be a perfume and an inspiration in the city and to the people among whom he lived. Those manly and tender graces in which he was so rich, the never-wearying unselfishness, the patient and benignant gentleness, — ah! shall we ever forget them? God forbid!

For to one at least who to-day recalls these rare and winning traits which so enriched and ennobled his personal character they will never cease to be a spell of most potent and pathetic power. I may not trust myself to speak of what I owe to him whom we have come here to mourn and to honor. I may not venture to give the rein to those deepest feelings of grateful love and veneration which are stirred in me by the memory of that pure and knightly manhood. Words are too poor for the expression of emotions which are intertwined with the deepest and most sacred affection; but you and I, — brethren beloved in the common Master! — you and I may well bless God for such a life, for such a work, for such a friend! Too short was that life and work, do we say? Yes, as the world measures life and work; but oh, how round and rich and complete in the best fruitage of Christian graces, of noble service, of a rare and royal manhood! Smitten, sorrowful, and bereaved, we must needs own ourselves; but happy the household, happy the diocese, happy the State and the nation, that have such a father and such a citizen and son! Tonight we hang his portrait — that kingly image of him who "from his shoulders upward," in every rarest grace and noblest quality, was loftier and kinglier than his fellows — high upon the wall of memory, and in the chamber of our deepest reverence. With that prophet of the elder time we look up, as the form of our friend and leader vanishes from our view, and cry, "My father, my father! the chariots of Israel and the horsemen thereof!" And then, translating the prayer of the lonely Elisha into our Christian speech, shall we not also cry, "O thou Mighty One, who wast to this thy departed servant Leader and Lord, let a double portion of his spirit, which was thy Spirit, be upon these his children and thine!"

NOTE. — In what is said here of the educational work of the Church, reference is had rather to the conditions under which such work has been undertaken than to the paramount importance of that work, concerning which there is, at any rate in the mind of the writer, not the smallest doubt. But the history of the University in our mother country may well instruct us in that which is the best wisdom in our own. Keble and Selwyn colleges have wisely been planted, not apart by themselves, as isolated schools of Church teaching and life, but close to great centres of education, with all their consequent advantages of libraries, lectures, and the stimulating atmosphere of a large and generous intellectual life. Our Church colleges have no less claim upon our sympathy and support, because in their beginnings the advantages of this course were not recognized. But, on the other hand, the wisdom which was first to see it must needs be owned. Churchmen owe it to good work always done, though not always perhaps in the wisest way, to "strengthen the things that remain." They owe it no less to work which yet remains to be done, to mix their doing of it with a frank recognition of the situation. — H. C. P.

Select Sermons.

BY SAMUEL SMITH HARRIS, D.D., LL.D.

Select Sermons.

SERMON I.

SHEPHERDHOOD.[1]

He that entereth in by the door is the shepherd of the sheep.—
St. John x. 2.

THE simple lesson which our Lord intended to teach in this familiar passage has often been strangely mistaken. The minds of men have been so fixed upon certain ecclesiastical conclusions which have been commonly derived from it, that the simpler but far profounder teaching which the Master had in mind to give has been overlooked. He was not defending the formal authority of his own or of any office. He was not discussing the regularity or lawfulness of his own or of any ministry. He was not pointing out the mode of entrance into shepherdhood, but he was telling how the function of all true shepherdhood must be discharged. He was laying down the rule

[1] Preached in St. Paul's Church, Detroit, Sunday morning, Sept. 21, 1879; being the first sermon delivered by Bishop Harris after his consecration as Bishop of Michigan.

of good conduct and right service in all true leadership, — a rule which He Himself exemplified and fulfilled, and which all must obey who hope in any degree to be worthy leaders of men.

Perhaps a brief examination of the context will enable us to apprehend our Lord's meaning a little more freshly. The term "shepherd" was commonly used among the Jews to denote the ruler or leader of the people. Such leaders the Pharisees claimed to be; and just before these words were uttered they had asserted their leadership in an exceedingly offensive fashion. Our Lord had opened the eyes of one who had been born blind; and the Pharisees, in attempting to persuade him that had been blind to deny the power of Jesus, had haughtily treated him as an altogether inferior being. When he replied, they reviled him for presuming to claim any sort of equality with themselves. "Thou wast altogether born in sin, and dost thou teach us?" So, when they were unable to use him for their purpose, they cast him out of the synagogue as one accursed. Our Lord beheld all this, and said in effect: "Do ye claim to be the shepherds of this people? I tell you nay: he that entereth not by the door into the sheepfold, but climbeth up some other way, the same is a thief and a robber; but he that entereth in by the door is the shepherd of the sheep." The fault which He denounced in them was that they did not identify themselves in work and sympathy with the people. The sheep enter in by the door into the sheepfold. The true shepherd enters in by the same door with the sheep. The Pharisees separated themselves from the people, climbing up some other way, and supposed that they were asserting and exercising their shepherdhood by their exclusiveness. But Jesus said, No; the true shepherd proves his shepherdhood, and realizes it by identifying himself with his flock, and entering in by the same lowly door with them. "He that entereth in by the door is the shepherd of the sheep."

It is perfectly obvious, then, that Jesus was not discussing the question of the credentials of authority, or of the formal commission of shepherdhood; but He was pointing out the only way in which shepherdhood of any kind can discharge its function and realize its power. He was propounding a lesson which it behooves all men to ponder well who hope to influence their fellow-men for good. Rank, office, order, culture, property,—be the authority, the privilege, the right of these what they may, the eternal law of God, as exemplified in the life of His Son, and taught in His Holy Word, and illustrated in human history, is this: that none of these, no matter how commissioned or sent, can exercise any real shepherdhood over men except as they are in sympathy with them. This is true in Church and State: of the employers of labor; of the heads of households; of civil rulers and political leaders; of bishops, priests, and deacons,—the power to lead men lies in sympathizing with them and walking in the same way with them. "He that entereth in by the door is the shepherd of the sheep." Saying this, the great Master spake not merely as a moralist and sage, but also as a statesman. He propounded a new principle in social and political economy which princes and diplomatists have hardly yet grown up to the grandeur of, though the vicissitudes of falling thrones and changing dynasties have been confirming it for thousands of years. For man has always been prone to think that eminence of gifts or station would give him power; that pomp or wealth or place would enable him to exercise dominion. But Jesus utterly reversed all this when He said, "Whosoever will be great among you, let him be your minister; and whosoever will be chief among you, let him be your servant: even as the Son of man came not to be ministered unto but to minister, and to give His life a ransom for many." Saying this He did not repudiate distinction of order, but rather pointed out the eternal purpose for which it is ordained. He did not renounce authority, but rather showed the only way to vindicate and exercise it. For He said in another place: "Ye call me Master and Lord: and ye say well; for so I am." But because I am your Lord and Master, I am among you as one that serveth. So here He taught the same great lesson. The man of influence is the man of sympathy; the man of power is the man of service. The shepherd enters in by the sheep's door; he leads them in and out and finds pasture for them. He knows them, and calls them by name. They know his voice, and will come when he calls them. He that walks with the sheep is the shepherd of the sheep.

Let us take the term "shepherd," then, in this its broadest signification. Let us think for a little while of shepherdhood as any kind of worthy leadership among men. Surely he that aspires to it in any walk of life entertains a noble ambition. Indeed, to have and to exert some kind of real influence over men is the only ambition that is worthy of a man. Give him any kind of power but this, clothe him with any other authority, and all that he has will be, without this, a weariness and a degradation. Let the widest proprietorship be assigned to him, let him claim the cattle on a thousand hills, let the rivers as they leap from the mountain and run to the sea not escape from his broad domains; yet the village Hampden who leads his rustic tenantry at the hustings, or the village poet who writes the songs which the people love to sing, may be a greater and more kingly soul than he. For the one is the lord of acres, the other is the ruler of souls. The one calls the hills and the fields his own, but the other moves and controls the immortal spirits of men. To do this worthily and well is a royal calling. To rule men is grander than to rule the stars in their courses; and to lead men is grander than to rule them. To lead men onward and upward, — this is to be a prince indeed: this is worthy of gentlemen and sons of God.

But how is such influence to be attained? How is such power to be won? To this the mere economist might say, "Get station or place; get official authority: that is power." But the answer is obvious. There is a distinction between the formal authority to lead men on the one hand and the power to lead them on the other; and the form of authority, to be effective, must be accompanied by the power. United, they constitute God's order for the guidance of the world: disunited, they stand as confusion on the one hand, and official incompetency on the other. Organization must be endowed with life to be efficient, and among men mere office-holding is not shepherdhood, mere station is not power.

The materialist might say, "Get money: that is power." But I answer, No, — not over the souls of men. It may command their hands or buy the product of their busy brains; but money, no matter how lavishly or how judiciously employed, cannot control the movements of the human heart.

Another would say, "Get knowledge: that is power." I answer, No: it may be power over the rivers and over the seas, over the lightnings and the clouds; it may summon the spirits of the air, like tricksy Ariels, to be its messengers, and use for its own purpose the leap of the cataract and the sweep of the storm; but something more than knowledge is required to rule men. It has no skill to touch the springs of human action, or to sweep the trembling chords of the human heart.

And so you may enumerate all the instrumentalities by means of which man has sought in time past or still seeks to rule, and as you tell them off, each must be rejected as powerless in the kingdom of souls, until we come at last to this great truth, which Christ uttered as the secret of the power of all true leadership and shepherdhood. He said, Sympathy with men is power over men. He that loves is he that leads. He that serves is he that rules. "He that entereth in by the door is the shepherd of the sheep."

Think now for a moment, and you will see why it must be so. Man is free. The soul is free in the truest, deepest sense of the word. God royally made it so, and even He cannot control it by any merely external force or power. It is free to think; it is free to will and choose; it is free to love; and no mere force or authority from without can control it in these operations in which its sovereign selfhood is realized. You may chain the limbs of a man, — you may coerce his actions or even his words; but how can you get into communion with the soul, and rule its will and its affections? There is only one way. If you would influence men intimately, profoundly, really, no matter what your authority or station, you must enter into sympathy with them. You must walk in the same path and enter in by the same door, or you can never be the shepherd of the sheep. This is what Saint Paul meant when he sang the praise of love. Among men love is power. "Though I speak with the tongues of men and of angels, . . . and though I have the gift of prophecy, and understand all mysteries, and all knowledge, and though I have all faith, so that I could remove mountains, . . . and though I bestow all my goods to feed the poor, and though I give my body to be burned, and have not *love*, it profiteth me nothing." And a greater than Saint Paul taught the same lesson and confirmed it by his own Divine experience. The Good Shepherd proved and illustrated His own Good Shepherdhood by sympathy and love. It was by no flash of splendor or miracle of external power that He proved His Divine leadership over the hearts of men; but by coming to walk with them, to toil and hunger and suffer with them. He entered into mortal life by the same lowly door of human birth; He passed through it by the same path of toil and daily care; He made His exit from it through the same portal of suffering and death. In life and death He walked with the sheep. Therefore He could say, "I am the good shepherd, not merely because I am commissioned and sent of my Father, not merely because I wield the power of omnipotence," but " I am the good shepherd," He said, because "I know my sheep and am known of mine." " The shepherd calleth his own sheep by name and leadeth them out. And when he putteth forth his own sheep, he goeth before them, and the sheep follow him, for they know his voice. He that walketh with the sheep, is the shepherd of the sheep."

The applications of this great principle are manifold, and extend to all the relations of life. It is the principle, in the first place, of all good government. The good ruler must be a shepherd, identifying himself, not in principle or opinion necessarily, but in sympathy with his people. Hence all good rulers, whether of high birth or low degree, whether kings like Victor Emmanuel or commoners like Washington or Lincoln, have all been men of the people. In precise proportion to the greatness and reality of their influence they have been shepherds every one.

So long as such rulers are content to be shepherds, walking with and leading their people, they retain their power; but the moment they begin to withdraw into privilege and prerogative they begin to lose it. While David sat daily in the gate to meet the people and right their wrongs, he ruled them, and they gave him a glad obedience. But when he withdrew into the exclusiveness of prerogative, the traitor Absalom came and stole their hearts away. So long as David relied on his shepherdhood, he reigned as a king; but when he forgot his shepherdhood and began to rely on his royalty, he lost his power, and came nigh losing his crown.

In this principle is to be found, moreover, the solution of the great social question of the day. The antagonism between labor and capital can be avoided; the rich and poor can be reconciled; intelligence and wealth can attain their rightful influence in the State and in society when intelligence and wealth enter into active sympathy with the poor. Let the rich and educated regard their wealth and intelligence as a sacred trust to be used in the service of their fellow-men; and then let them identify themselves in sympathy with the masses, and *they* will be the trusted leaders of the masses. Not otherwise; for the poor are just like other men. They are going to follow their *shepherds*, — those who walk with them and sympathize with them. And until the rich and intelligent in this free land become sufficiently Christianized to so identify themselves with the poor, they are not going to lead them. " He that entereth in by the door is the shepherd of the sheep."

But above all, this principle defines the mission of the Church of God. Venerable as she is above all the institutions of time, of Divine origin and appointment, clothed with authority from on high, set to be the witness and keeper of the truth, and commissioned to transmit it to the remotest generation, we who know and love her, yield to her divine authority our glad obedience. Yet the Church is more than a witness and keeper of the truth; she is more than a teacher sent from God; she is more than a divinely appointed polity to be perpetuated, or a divinely instituted authority to be respected and enforced. She is sent to scatter abroad the gifts of grace; to be the instrumentality in time of Him who, though unseen, is still the Good Shepherd. He works with her hands, He speaks with her voice, and it is still the Shepherd's voice, calling His own sheep by name, and leading them to the green pastures and beside the still waters. Were I asked, then, what is the chief manward function of the Church of God, I would say, Shepherdhood over the souls of men;

shepherdhood toward all whom Christ came to seek and to save; shepherdhood not merely toward those which are safely folded, but toward the lost and scattered sheep which stray bewildered upon the dark mountains; to realize on earth the will and the prayer of Him who not only said, "I am the good shepherd," but who also said, "Other sheep I have, which are not of this fold; them also must I bring, and they shall hear my voice; and there shall be one fold, and one shepherd."

But above all, the true shepherd must be a man of that genuine sensibility of soul that feels all that concerns his fellow-men; that feels their sorrows, shares their joys, instinctively divines their difficulties, generously shares their burdens. This is the distinguishing characteristic of all great Christian leaders, and in this is the hiding of their power. Such sympathy cannot be simulated; it is impossible to play a part in this. A man must have a genuine respect and a genuine affection for men as men, or he cannot be their shepherd. At the remarkable meeting that was held some two years ago at Westminster Abbey to take steps for erecting a monument to the late Dean Stanley, it was said by more than one of the speakers who knew him well, that the secret of his remarkable power over men was his many-sided sympathy. He was a genuine lover of his kind. He loved men as men; not for what they had, nor for what they thought, nor for what they did; but he loved them, regardless of class or creed, as men. It was a wondrous and precious gift; and he used it so that when he died there were three continents that mourned him, though there were few of those who mourned him that altogether agreed with him. So of the great dean it is not too much to say that it was not his learning, nor his rank, nor his riches, nor his presence, that made him a great shepherd-hearted prophet, for such he undoubtedly was; but it was his humble walk with God, and his many-sided sympathy with his kind. In the minds and hearts of many thousands who utterly differed from him, this redeemed his mistakes; and he is already numbered among the illustrious abbots of Westminster, among the worthies of England, among the great shepherd-prophets of the Anglo-Saxon race.

You will pardon me, my brethren, if I venture to say in this, my first public utterance among you, that it is with thoughts like these that I have prayed to come to begin my ministry here: to be in some humble measure, but oh, in Christ's deep and lowly sense, a servant of my brethren; to take heed unto the flock over which the Holy Ghost hath made me overseer; to strive to know the sheep and call them by name; to lead them forth, and to have the sheep know my voice and come at my calling. And this it is to be a shepherd indeed; this it is to be a bishop of souls in the church of God, — not to be ministered unto, but to minister. This is the divine rule of headship; and oh, may it be mine as I go in and out among you!

But it is not alone of myself that I would speak,

or even chiefly of myself. You and I are all called, each in our station and degree, to help make this dear old Church of ours, which God hath sent to this Western land, realize her high vocation, and be a shepherd church to all this mighty people, by leading in every good word and work, by showing the world that there is nothing good that we have not a sympathy with, by doing all that in us lies to bring them back to the old path, and to lead them in the better way by the kindly ministries of gentleness and love; to teach an alienated people to see in the Church itself a shepherd's care, and to hear a shepherd's voice. To do this is to be true teachers in the Church of God. And you and I are called to be shepherds as individuals in our places and in our separate vocations. Every father and every mother, every employer of labor, and every head of a household ought to remember this. It is a great privilege, that of being the guides and leaders of men, — in this way to be shepherds in the Israel of God.

One summer morning a traveller was standing upon the side of a mighty mountain. A beautiful lake spread out before him, casting back like a mirror the flood of golden sunlight that fell upon it, while above his head the morning mists were weaving a fantastic coronet to crown the king of the mountains. As he stood there drinking in the beauty, he saw a shepherd of that country pass along the pathway by a brook, leading a flock of sheep to a higher and greener pasture that was above on the side of the mountain. The traveller called to the shepherd and said, "Give me your hand, and come up over the rock, for you will get wet as you walk along the pathway!" But he said, " Na, na; the sheep canna climb the rock, and they wadna stan' still gin I clum up there. I mun gang before the sheep, gin I wad lead them!" And the traveller said: "This, then, is shepherdhood, — shepherdhood like that of Moses, or Joshua, or Paul, or Selwyn, or Coleridge Patterson, or like the shepherdhood of our own beloved leaders of the flock who have entered into their rest. This is true shepherdhood, — not to climb up some other way, but to walk before the sheep." Oh, brethren, may such a shepherdhood be yours and mine, and so may it be our privilege to keep around us and about us all those whom we love! And as our springtime flows into summer, and our summer begins to languish into autumn and winter, may it be our blessed privilege to lead them higher and higher up the mountain-side where the greener pastures are, till at last we shall come to see the gloriously fashioned door of the heavenly fold swinging open to admit us and those we bring with us, its golden hinges turning and gleaming in the light of the everlasting Sun, what time we begin to catch, as the sounds of this world die away, the sweeter voices trained to know the Good Shepherd's voice, and He shall come forth to meet us and lead us into the green pastures and beside the still waters, to bask forever and forever beneath the smile of God.

SERMON II.

THE DIGNITY OF MAN.[1]

And God said, Let us make man in our image, after our likeness: and let them have dominion over the fish of the sea, and over the fowl of the air, and over the cattle, and over all the earth, and over every creeping thing that creepeth upon the earth. So God created man in his own image, in the image of God created he him. — GEN. i. 26, 27.

A GREAT poet has profoundly said that "the proper study of mankind is man." It is a truth which all generations of thinking men have need to recognize and ponder; for a right estimate of what man is and may become lies at the foundation of all social and political philosophy. I count it one of the peculiar misfortunes of our day and time that this noble study has been so much neglected. For more than a generation the tendency

[1] Preached in St. Paul's Church, Detroit, on the morning of the first Sunday in Advent, 1884. Preached also in St. Thomas Church, Winchester, England, on Sunday morning, July 15, 1888. This was the last sermon delivered by Bishop Harris, and the one during which he had that momentary unconsciousness which was the beginning of his last illness. It was described in a letter from the Rev. Arthur H. Sole, as follows: "He preached us a noble sermon, 'Let us make man in our image,' etc., and he dwelt upon man's infinite possibilities of good, and his potential power. When he had preached for about fifteen minutes, he suddenly became silent, and for a moment I felt most anxious. Then he braced himself with an effort, and finished his sermon entirely without manuscript, in a manner that touched and helped us all."

of human thought has been in a different direction. The wonderful development of a material civilization has engrossed the attention and absorbed the energy of the race. In the midst of steam-enginery, human agency has seemed to be of less account. The machine has seemed in large degree to supplant the man. The study of things and not of ideas, of relations and not of principles, of forms and combinations and not of the power which sustains them, have made the age in which we live, with all its splendor of material achievement, a superficial age, in which the true dignity of the soul and the true sanctities of human life are often obscured and forgotten. To this is due in large part the notorious decay of statesmanship; the shallowness of our contemporary thinking; the empiricism which is the reproach of our professions; the desecration of home and of marriage; the alienation of classes and the disregard of human rights and human duties, which are likely at any time to lead to conflict and disaster. For this, the only remedy is to call men back to a sense of what their true interests are; and the first step in this process must be a return to a true estimate of man's dignity and destiny. For man is the lord of all beneath him, and the witness for all above him, designed to be earth's sovereign and God's likeness; and unless we know him in some real sense we cannot understand the world or time, to say nothing of eternity and God.

But beyond all question a right estimate of what man is and may become must lie at the foundation of all religious philosophy. It is therefore altogether in the line of my duty as chief pastor of souls, that I ask you to begin with me this morning a brief study of man's dignity and destiny. From this we will pass, on next Sunday morning, to a study of the indignity and enormity of that sin which so dishonors and debases man's regal and aspiring nature; and then to the wonder and the power of redemption, through which this foul dishonor is done away; and finally to the joy of that eternal life which beginning here shall last forever. Our subject this morning, then, shall be man's dignity and destiny; and for a text I turn to this venerable record of human history which tells us of man's beginning, by what power and in what image he was fashioned, and into what likeness he was designed to grow. "And God said, Let us make man in our image, after our likeness. . . . So God created man in his own image, in the image of God created he him."

It is no part of my present purpose to discuss the manner of man's creation. As Christians we need not be at all disturbed if in the course of scientific investigation it should be established that man as a physical being is the result of a long process of evolution, — the same process through which all the rest of the physical universe has been builded. The grandeur of God's creative act would not be obscured, but only enhanced, were we to-day to regard it not as having been exercised in a moment or by a single fiat, but as extending through ages of development, beginning with primordial forces and monad forms, and ending with man as the crown and consummate flower of creation. The theory of evolution is not yet proved. There are many scientific philosophers among the very greatest, like Professor Agassiz, who believe that it never can be established. But even if it should be established as the true account of man's origin as a physical being, it will not be in conflict with religious truth, or with the true meaning of this Divine Word. For man is more than a physical being. No matter from what standpoint we regard him, we find in him what no physical philosophy can pretend to account for. In him we find certain characteristic faculties and powers which mark him as wholly distinct from all other creatures on this earth of ours; and these characteristic faculties and powers are the differentia of man as an intellectual, moral, and spiritual being. In the great transaction of man's creation, then, whether it was evolutionary or instantaneous, there was an epoch-marking moment when a new factor appeared; when a new and supernal entity made its august appearance as a visitant from another world; when a power from on high for the first time touched the organic and material, and took up its abode in this lower world, — and that was the supreme moment when God breathed the breath of life into man's nostrils, and he became a living soul. And when we study that soul we find that it bears the impress of its divine origin; that it was fashioned not according to any earthly pattern, but after a pattern in the heavens. We read without wonder that it was not in the image of any brutish existence that man's soul was fashioned, but that it was fashioned in the image of God. And this was done not without deliberate counsel and purpose. We are struck, in reading this ancient narrative, with the difference between this act and all that preceded it. All former things seem to have arisen, as it were, in accordance with some easy and natural plan, — the light, the firmament, the fishes, the cattle, the birds. But when it came to the creation of man, the council of the eternal Godhead was solemnly convoked. The sublime purpose of reproducing here on earth a being in the image of the invisible God was meditated and announced. After the pattern of Godhead the soul's manhood was fashioned and made, and the great fact is here recorded. "So God created man in his own image; in the image of God created he him."

Therefore it is that the soul is the man; in man's mental, moral, and spiritual nature his true manhood lies. In this world man has a body, but he is a soul. And the soul is the real man. Undoubtedly man's physical nature is useful and necessary here. With all its frailties it constitutes a splendid equipment for the human spirit. All creation moved by steady gradation upward to man as a physical being, and in him it reached its summit and consummation. It is one of the latest and most authoritative announcements of the evolutionary school of scientific thinkers, that man is not only the loftiest and noblest product of evolution, but that he is and shall be the last; that in him the principle of natural selection has given place to another law which has forever closed the ascending series of species, and that there can be, therefore, no nobler creation on this earth of ours than man. And when we consider man merely as a physical being, how matchless he is! Erect and free, his very attitude is that of lordship. What a piece of work he is! in form and moving how express and admirable, — a front like Jove himself; an eye like Mars to threaten and command! Who shall say or sing the marvels of the " human face divine"? who shall imitate the wonders of the human hand? In all the boundless range of art its skill gives form to human thought and makes it glow on canvas or breathe in marble. It wields the flashing sword in battle, and soothes the fevered brow of pain; it fells the giant oak, and by its clasp cements the bond of friendship; it is the instrument of power, of love, and of blessing. And then the voice of man, — the organs of speech, the power to make articulate sounds and fashion them into words, those airy messengers which tell the secret thoughts of soul to soul, which make up that marvellous thing called language. And yet even these powers belong to the physical man only because he has a soul within him. They are simply the agents by means of which the soul expresses itself and holds communion with the outer world.

Man's true nature, then, — that which constitutes his true manhood, — is mental, moral, spiritual; that which belongs to him in distinction from all other beings known to him here; which makes him what he is,—a man. As such he is able to apprehend the environment by which he is conditioned, and to look through it to a higher state of existence. As such he is able to will what is right and to choose what is good. As such he is able to love the ideal and so to rise toward it. In a word, his manhood is his personality, his individuality as an intellectual, moral, and spiritual being.

It is a stupendous fact that every soul is unique in its inmost personality. Each differs from every other, stands in its own lot, bears its own burden, goes to its own place alone. The law of generation, transmission, inheritance, largely shapes and determines man's physical nature; but the soul's individuality is original and underived. The reason is that every soul is a fresh creation. The body is begotten through generation: the soul of each child that is born comes direct from the creative power of God. I cannot take time now to discuss the question between Traducianists, who assert that the souls, like the bodies of all men, are derived through generation from Adam, and the Creationists, who assert that while the physical nature is so derived, each soul is a separate creation. Suffice it that the last view is the only view that is tenable. Beyond all question the new-created soul is conditioned by its environment. Enshrined in a body that inherits evil, the soul is conditioned by that evil; hence we have original sin, inherited tendency, transmitted bias, and other peculiarities of temperament and temper. But the fact remains that each soul, however conditioned by its body, is the result of a fresh creative act, and comes directly from the power and love of God. With Wordsworth, therefore, we can say, —

> "Our birth is but a sleep and a forgetting :
> The soul that rises with us, our life's star,
> Hath had elsewhere its setting,
> And cometh from afar.
> Not in entire forgetfulness,
> And not in utter nakedness,
> But trailing clouds of glory, do we come
> From God, who is our home."

Therefore it is that in spite of all the associations that entangle him here, man is the master of his own destiny. No matter how squalid the environment of his birth, nor how low and ignoble the lot to which he is born; no matter how unknown or unworthy the name which he inherits, or what swarthy hues barbaric suns may have burned into the cheeks of his ancestors, the soul of every man is a new creation by God, and ought to be free and equal among his fellow-men. It is in this fact that I read the charter of human rights and human freedom. In this I discern the falseness of all class distinctions and other barriers that would separate man from man. In the kingdom of souls there are no inherited degrees of honor or shame. Each is free, and fully entitled to the place which he can honestly win and honorably hold. Therefore man is a responsible being. He comes into the world a sovereign soul, with power to determine the quality of his own life and action. And this responsibility he cannot abdicate any more than he can obliterate his own individuality. He cannot ease himself of it or share it with another.

There is infinite pathos and pitifulness in the thought of man's lonely individuality, but there is grandeur too. In the solitude of its individuality each soul is a crowned and sceptred king. Day by day and hour by hour he must determine the awful issues of right and wrong, of life and death, as they arise, and no man and no angel can interpose between him and his dread responsibility. In a deep and real sense he must think and choose and live out his life alone, even as he must go alone through the dark valley and shadow of death to that judgment which shall disclose what manner of man he has made himself to be in the sovereign freedom of his soul.

In this sovereign individuality, then, man is endowed with those original powers which he must exercise, for the right exercise of which he is responsible, and in the right exercise of which his true dignity lies, — the power to know, the power to will or choose, and the power to love. And first, of the power to know. It is a great truth that in man the world first became conscious of itself. No being lower than man is able to take cognizance of the world's meaning, to drink in its beauty, to appropriate its good. Man only is able, through observation and reflection, to understand the laws of nature and the sequence of history. He only can discern and appropriate creation's power and joy, — the mountain's grandeur, the landscape's beauty the majesty of night, the glory of day. For him the aurora spreads its fitful light and the rainbow lifts its lovely form; for him the morning blushes in gladness over the eastern mountains, and the day departs with splendor through the portals of the western sky. For him the flowers bloom, and all the beautiful things of earth, — not for the beasts which see and heed them not, but for man, for the angels, and for God. Fast as his knowledge expands his power grows. He makes the rivers and the seas his highways, the lightnings his messengers, the winds and the currents and all Nature's forces his servants, because he alone has the power to understand and therefore to use them. Not only so, but from them he is able to reason to higher things, — to look into the mirror of his own soul, to read the majestic secrets that are reflected there; and so, being conscious of the world and of himself, to become conscious of God. 'T is the power to know, which is the signature of divinity in the soul of man. The quest for knowledge is a divine quest, the soul that engages in it is exercising one of the royal prerogatives of its nature, and all true seekers after truth are seekers after God.

Next, man has the power to will, to choose freely between good and evil. Perhaps of all his powers this is the most characteristic of him as a man, for the brute has no such power. The brute is under the absolute control of instinct. When an object of fear or desire is placed before a brute, it instinctively seizes it or flies from it; but man has a peculiar power of determining his own actions for himself, and of choosing freely between right and wrong. Passion may say it is desirable or undesirable, appetite may say it is fair or repulsive, but conscience whispers it is right or wrong, and man has power to heed conscience in defiance of passion and appetite; to say, "I'll do right at whatever cost;" to say, "I'll do this thing, not because of fear or desire, but because it is right, and I'll refuse to do that thing because it is wrong." The power to do this belongs of right to every soul. No squalid surroundings at birth have ever been able to banish it, no inherited languor or taint in the blood has ever been able to steal it away. The man himself may sin it away; but until it is forfeited by his own mad act it belongs to every soul. And this it is which makes the soul of man so great; which makes man greater than all the universe besides, for all things else are in bondage to necessary law. The wandering comet is held in the firm leash of law, as is also the wild hurricane that sweeps across continents and careers over foaming seas. The iron hand of necessity hurls the cataract and paints the lily and shakes the aspen in the breeze. In all the world there is only one thing that is free, and that is the soul of man. No external force or power, no inherited tendency or bias, can coerce his thought, his choice, his affection. Made in God's image, he alone can wield this sovereign, this godlike power, and act not from instinct, or caprice, or impulse, or passion, or any kind of necessity, but freely do the right because it is right. This is the characteristic power and glory of a man.

Finally, another characteristic of the human soul is the power to love the ideal; this too is part of the equipment of a sovereign nature. Not passion, or desire, or longing, or any sickly sentimentalism, but the outgoing of man's affection from himself toward an ideal beauty or grace, in a generous, noble, unselfish desire to honor and bless that ideal, — this is human love. It is the inspiration of all noble endeavor, the principle of all aspiration, the spirit of all worship. This power, strongest in the strong, noblest in the noble, has been the secret of all real advancement among men, — the power to love and so to approach the ideal beauty, goodness, grace; in a word, the power to love God. Time fails me to speak of it to-day as I would. Let it suffice now to say that this is pre-eminently man's spiritual faculty. Blindly, fitfully, it often gropes and even grovels here, wasting its wealth of tenderness often on objects most unworthy; but its highest earthly exercise is Christian worship, its loftiest fruition will be the beatific vision when man shall see the King in His beauty, and behold the land that is very far off.

Can you not now divine for yourselves the great lesson to which our thought has conducted us? Man's true dignity lies in the right use of these noble faculties which constitute the equipment of his nature. I know indeed that this regal nature of his is fallen. On Sunday next I am to speak of the indignity wrought upon man and within him by sin. But even in his fallen state, all man's grandeur lies in what he is and may become. And if to the idea of dignity we add the idea of worth, then he who has most nobly used these regal faculties of his soul is the man of most dignity and most worth. And the noblest use of these faculties is that which directs them to what is above man, not to what is beneath him; to what pertains to his soul's everlasting interest, and not the perishable interests of time and sense. To know the Truth, to choose the Right, to love the Infinite Good, — this is man's true vocation. I know that there are interests that belong to man's earthly estate. It is part of his high calling to subdue the world and exercise dominion over it, and this he can do only by the labor of business, the travail of thought, the toil of enterprise and discovery. The man who fails to do his share toward the attainment or the rectification of this dominion, having no adequate disability to excuse him, is a laggard or a coward in life's battle. But let not the man who succeeds in winning the world make the fatal mistake of supposing that this is all. Not earth only, but heaven also, is to be won. And in the winning of earthly success the sole value of all his enterprise and toil to his undying soul is not what he gets to have, but what he gets to be. The supreme question is, With all my gain am I gaining wisdom, and with all my getting am I getting understanding? "For the merchandise of it is better than the merchandise of silver, and the gain thereof than fine gold."

And oh, if men could only understand this, how much easier would it be to bear what men call earthly misfortune or earthly failure! How evident it is that these when honestly encountered and bravely borne are the choicest conditions for winning the true success of the soul, the true grace of manhood, which is likeness to God!

In a vision once I seemed to know a proud people who dwelt in a goodly land. Bright skies bent above it, summer seas breathed upon it, and careless plenty abounded in the homes of "fair women and brave men." And I seemed to see a cloud of war arise and hang like a meteor upon the declivities of the mountains. Then the storm broke and surged over that fair land. Not a home but was bereaved, not a woman in all its congregations but was draped in mourning. Desolation stalked through all its borders. And then after years of untold anguish came utter defeat, utter failure, utter poverty, utter ruin. The years passed on, — years of such humiliation and suffering as we in our waking moments can hardly understand. And then the fruits, the peaceable fruits of those years of grievous chastening seemed to appear, — such grace and tenderness and sweet humility, such piety in young and old, as never existed in the old days of that people's prosperity, and such as shall, if not lost through sin and folly, make the homes of that people a praise through all the earth. Which vision I take to be an allegory wherein to read the great lesson that it is not in what he has, nor in what he boasts, but in what he is, that man's true worth is to be found; and even misfortune and disaster and failure are transformed into blessing and success, if through them the soul is humbled and strengthened and more conformed to the likeness of God. Surely it is hard enough to compass this in the midst of earthly chastening; but to grow more and more unworldly in the midst of worldly prosperity, — *hic labor, hoc opus est*. But whether in wealth or adversity, God's grace is freely offered to us, redeeming Love has opened the way for us, atoning mercy stretches down a Saviour's hand to help us.

Nay, the Spirit of God is now freely offered to help our infirmities, to restore the Divine image in our souls, to guide us into all truth, to enable us to choose the right, to love the good, and so to rise to a likeness to God.

SERMON III.

THE INDIGNITY OF SIN.[1]

But he that sinneth against me wrongeth his own soul : all they that hate me love death. — PROV. viii. 36.

IN one of the most remarkable passages in epic literature the poet Milton describes the meeting of Satan, Sin, and Death at the gate of hell. Of Sin and Death he says: —

> " Before the gates there sat
> On either side a formidable shape;
> The one seemed woman to the waist, and fair;
> But ended foul in many a scaly fold
> Voluminous and vast; a serpent armed
> With mortal sting: About her middle round
> A cry of hell-hounds never ceasing barked
> With wide Cerberean mouths full loud, and rung
> A hideous peal; . . .
>   The other shape,
> If shape it might be called that shape had none
> Distinguishable in member, joint, or limb;
> Or substance might be called that shadow seemed,
> For each seemed either; black it stood as night,
> Fierce as ten furies, terrible as hell,
> And shook a dreadful dart; what seemed his head
> The likeness of a kingly crown had on."

Then follows, in Milton's great epic, a description of the meeting between the arch-fiend and

[1] Preached in St. Paul's Church, Detroit, on the morning of the second Sunday in Advent, 1884.

these horrible shapes, of the imminent conflict, the sudden recognition, the final reconciliation, and then of the opening of the gates of hell by the keys of death, and of the sallying forth of these malignant powers to vex and destroy the human race. And when we look upon the course of human history we seem to see a direful confirmation of the poet's story. As if in very deed sin and death had issued forth from hell's yawning portals, and had indeed come hither to work their woful will, we seem to see in all man's manifold wretchedness the evidence of a fiendish power too subtle and too malignant to be of earth. For thrice two thousand years these loathsome shapes have seemed to walk this earth of ours, the one sowing, the other reaping, while all creation has groaned and travailed, as if smitten with a curse.

We need not invoke the aid, however, of the poet's gloomy fancy to deepen our sense of the awfulness of human misery. The most appalling fact with which human experience has to deal is the existence of evil. Fair as is the world in which we live, this is the shadow that haunts all its visions of splendor. Joyous as each generation is as it sets out in the glee of childhood and the gladness of youth, this is the woe that dogs its footsteps and saddens all its mirth. In Nature itself, as if in secret sympathy with man, there seems to be, in the falling leaves and the sobbing winds of autumn, and in the moan of the waves as they break on solitary shores, the bodeful sense of evil. And that evil seems to confront and

threaten us with dark and unearthly malignity, in
the coil of the serpent, the roar of the beast, and
the strident shriek of the storm. And when we
turn from Nature to the haunts of men, we en-
counter the same sense of the presence and malignity of evil. Society itself may be said to live
in an embattled camp, guarded by sentinels who
perpetually stand to their arms. Courts, jails, and
prisons, policemen, bailiffs, and other myrmidons
of the law, the locks upon the doors of our houses,
the lights that burn by night in our streets, are all
witnesses of the felt presence of evil against which
it behooves men to guard themselves and those
whom they love. Not only so, but these tell not
half the story. There is a deeper, darker, deadlier
evil than courts and magistrates can deal with and
punish. Far down in the depths of man's being
is the fell disorder of which all guilty acts are but
the symptoms and outward manifestations; and
that dread disorder is sin. What a terrible thing
it is! How boundless, how unutterable the ill that
it has wrought! Not a home in all the world that
has not been darkened by it; not a family that has
not been bereaved; not a life that has not been
burdened and saddened by it. All the groans
that agonizing humanity has uttered; all the sighs
that have been sobbed out of aching hearts; all
the tears that men, women, and children have
shed; all real sorrow, all real woe, have sprung
from that terrible thing called Sin, the mother of
Death.

I do not intend this morning to inquire into the

dark question of the origin of evil. As you know, it is around this problem that the most subtle, the most eager, and the most bootless of all theological controversies have raged. It is not necessary to our present purpose that we should renew or review the wordy strife. It will be enough for us to begin with the postulate, that the possibility of sin was involved in man's freedom as a moral being, and that the actuality of sin resulted from the abuse of that freedom. In his sovereign counsel God decreed that man should be made in his own image, and should therefore be a moral being. But he could not be a moral being unless he should be free; he could not be free without liberty of choice; he could not have liberty of choice unless the better and the worse should be present to him; and in choosing between them he chose the worse instead of the better, and the result was sin and death. Through man's freedom, then, sin came into the world, and death by sin. This much suffices for us to know. There remains the question, however, What is sin; and how is it related to the soul and its life?

For our present purpose it will not be sufficient to say with Saint John that sin is the transgression of the law, or that all unrighteousness is sin; nor with Saint Paul that sin is the negation of faith, so that whatsoever is not of faith is sin. Profoundly true as these answers are, yet a little reflection is necessary to enable us to appropriate their truth. We must first recur, then, to the thought of what man is, and of what his relation was intended to be to the world and time, to eternity and God. We have seen, then, that man is essentially and characteristically a spiritual being; that it is his intellectual, moral, and spiritual nature that distinguishes him from all other creatures known to him here, and that this it is which makes him what he is,—a man. Man, then, is a soul, and the soul is the real man. In this state of existence, however, man has a body; and body and soul are so intimately united that they constitute the living person. Through his physical nature, then, man is related to the world and time, just as through his spiritual nature he is related to eternity and God. But in this complex being, man's physical nature was intended to be in all things obedient and subordinate, the instrument and servant of his nobler part; because his spiritual nature is his true nature, and his physical nature is common to him with the brutes that perish. By the faculties of his nobler nature, moreover, man exercises all the nobler functions of his being, taking cognizance of the meaning of the world and of time, of ideas, of thoughts, of beauty, of goodness, of God. But the faculties of man's physical nature deal only with the phenomena of time and sense, revealing to him only what the very brutes can see and feel and love. Now, it was man's temptation, that while the higher world was accessible to him through these powers of his nobler nature, the lower world was making its insidious appeal to him through sense; and his fall consisted in his yielding to this enchantment, and so giving his soul's allegiance to the objects of sense. The choice came before him so that to choose the lower was to reject the higher; to follow appetite was to forsake duty; to believe the tempter was to deny God. He made the fatal choice. The moment he did so, the harmony of his nature was broken up, and his life swung from its true centre. The part of his nature that was intended to be servant became master. The world that was intended to obey him became his lord. Time, that was intended to be but the season of his tutelage, seemed to span and include his whole existence; and all the glad sense of immortality and of God was extinguished by guilty fear and earthliness. In a word, man began to become *flesh*, and all his higher nature to be foully dishonored. The law of life which had reigned in his soul became subordinate to the law of death which reigned in his mortal members; and the confusion, the shame, the dishonor which then began in the soul is the awful condition of heart and life which we call *sin*. Now, then, there are various definitions of sin, each one of which is true according to our standpoint. If we regard sin as a violation of man's true destiny, which destiny we read not only in God's loving command, but also in the very law of man's own being, then sin is the transgressing of the law. If we regard sin as variation from the right, the good, the true, then sin is unrighteousness. If we regard sin as the negation of man's true nature as a spiritual being, and the identifying of him with the things of sense, then sin is materialism. If we regard sin as the fixing of the affections — affections that were intended for glories beyond the stars — upon the perishing things of this world, then sin is worldliness. And finally, if we regard sin as the failure or refusal of the soul to apprehend and confide in the unseen, then sin is unbelief. In the sphere of law, then, sin is transgression; in the sphere of morals, it is unrighteousness; in the sphere of thought, it is materialism; in the sphere of conduct, it is worldliness; in the sphere of spiritual apprehension, it is unbelief. But it is always the one and selfsame thing, the same grim and ghastly thing, — in the godless man of the world, and the ruffian who outrages law, and the smooth libertine and vulgar thief; in the respectable atheist who says there is no God, and the brave outlaw who lives his creed and acts upon his belief. For we must remember that while sins differ, sin, the evil root out of which all sins proceed, is the same. Sins are but symptoms: the disease called sin lies deeper in the soul. You may hide or even suppress the symptoms, and yet the sin may be as deadly and ghastly as ever. For instance, the sinner may not steal, but he may covet; he may not murder, but he may hate; and in all such cases, though there be no outward act, the sin may be the same in the heart. And oh, it is an awful thought, well calculated to humble us all into the very dust, that no matter what our sins may be, — no matter how decent, how respectable, how secret, — they each and all proceed out of the same fell disorder as the sins of the veriest wretch who outrages man's laws and exhausts man's patience by his wickedness! In all cases the sin at bottom is the same, whether it be called transgression, unrighteousness, materialism, worldliness, or unbelief.

And now that sin has been traced to its last analysis, let us consider its results on the soul. It was Wisdom that of old spoke the words of my text, and her voice is still uplifted among the sons of men: "He that sinneth against me wrongeth his own soul." It is true that he wrongs the souls of others also. No man ever sins but he inflicts a grievous wrong upon some other soul; it may be upon many. It may be an everlasting woe upon multitudes of souls, both here and hereafter. Oh, if we could only understand that awful truth, — the persistency of evil! The evil word, the unfeeling jest, the cold and brutal sneer, the wicked example, once done or said, go forth dealing death, — may go down the ages dealing woe upon thousands of souls long after the wicked or heedless heart that did the wrong lies mouldering in the grave. But it is not of this that I now speak. The worst wrong, the deepest indignity, is done to the soul that commits the sin. "He that sinneth against me wrongeth his own soul."

And first, he wrongs his soul by the degradation he inflicts upon it, the evil that he scatters through it. The soul comes as a new creation from God. It is enshrined in a body that inherits evil, — evil propensities, insurgent affections; and it has a hard struggle at best, and cannot win the victory but by the help of God. But the man who sins makes a voluntary surrender of the nobler to the baser part, and so appropriates the frailty of the baser nature, and makes it a part of his soul's being. Each sin by a certain reflex action spreads disorder through man's whole nature. In this way the very bodily appetite may become the appetite also of the soul. Oh, grim and ghastly are the evils which sin inflicts upon the body! It dulls the eye, and palsies the hand, and banishes manly grace from the brow, and coarsens and brutalizes the human face divine. Disease, decrepitude, frailty, are among the dread indignities that sin often works upon the body. But something far more dreadful than this befalls the sinner. The soul takes on the vice of the body. The worst symptom of drunkenness, for instance, is not the craving of the body, but the craving of the soul. The soul of the inebriate begins to crave the false excitement of drink, and an obliquity corresponding to that of the body begins to be set up in the soul. The eye of the drunkard sees false or sees double: the mind's eye begins to see false also. And so it comes to pass that the soul of the drunkard becomes untruthful. It is now well known that men who habitually get drunk will lie. This is the reason that men cannot trust the word of a drunkard. So also the deadly sin of impurity. The very mind and conscience become defiled. The mind becomes pander to the body. Oh, horrible degradation! And so we find that there is a correspondence and correlation between different kinds of sin. The sensual man is always a cruel man. The drunkard is a liar. The thief is simply covetous and selfish, just like the worldling and the miser. In all these things man's whole nature is shamed and dishonored. In all his being he is degraded and coarsened by his sin.

And this becomes all the more evident when we examine the wrong which sin does to man's characteristic powers. And first, his intellectual faculties, his reason, his power to know. It is a great and awful truth, little heeded, little understood, that all the powers of man's intellect are blunted and weakened by sin. That this should be so lies in the very nature of things. Man's regal mind cannot be overpowered by appetite or passion without grievous debasement and deterioration. Who has not seen the splendor of some lordly intellect first dimmed, then obscured, by excess or folly, until its fitful light would blaze out only at intervals, and then go out in piteous darkness, or fade into still more pitiable imbecility? But even more pitiable, if possible, is it to see the royal intellect of man forced into the base service of the world, and compelled to drudge like a very slave in the interest of sordid vice, or avarice, or other selfishness. Who does not know how such intellect declines into trickery or beastly cunning, as it watches like a fox for a chance to deceive, or like a predatory beast to seize its prey? To such a man high thoughts and noble purposes become simply impossible. While others do the noble deeds and carry out the beneficent plans of life, he is intent simply on selfish gratifications; is pampering his little pride, or seeking his little pleasure, or heaping together his sordid gains, and so growing more and more insensible to the call of honor and reason, more and more base, and more and more contemptible.

Not less disastrous, not less dishonoring, is the influence of sin on man's moral nature, — on his power to discriminate and choose between right and wrong. Of the debilitating effect of sin upon the will of man I need not speak at length. All observation and all experience prove that this is its immediate, unvarying, inevitable effect. He who once yields to do wrong will find it harder the next time to do right, until he speedily becomes powerless to choose good and resist evil. But of the darkening, paralyzing effect of sin upon a moral sense not so much is commonly thought, though such effect is not less immediate and inevitable. The moral sense, which at first is quick to discriminate, begins, under the pressure of sin, to lose the keenness of perception. The high sense of honor and of truthfulness is dulled. The good seems to be less good, and the evil does not seem to be so very evil, until at last that soul calls evil good, and good evil. Woe to the soul that is in such a case! Woe to him that puts darkness for light and light for darkness! He has abdicated his throne, and lost his regal state, and broken his sceptre, and flung away his crown. Such a desperate degradation is not reached all at once, — not till years of sin, it may be, and of indulgence have passed by. But let the soul remember that the first sin is the first step, and that the next will be easier, and that with each succeeding sin the momentum increases at a fearful rate until its speed shall hurl it down to ruin.

Finally, even more debasing is the effect of sin upon the affections. This would seem to be the worst degradation of all, — that man should not only sin his intellect and will and conscience away, but that he should love his shame, that his soul should be enamoured of its degradation. And yet, who does not know that even this is the effect of sin? Through it men learn to love the base things of this world, and lose the power to love the nobler things. What is life to such a soul but shame? What shall death be but the beginning of an eternal bereavement? All its affections are fixed on things of sense. All its delights and all its joys are bound up with the pleasures of sense. And when death comes and strips off the pampered flesh, and the world, which alone it is able to love, fades away like the baseless fabric of a vision, what shall eternity be to that soul but an eternal bereavement of all that it is able to love, and therefore an eternal torture and an eternal death?

One word in conclusion. All the effects of sin upon the soul may be summed up in one dreadful word, and that is *Death*. There is indeed a phantom called by that name, and he too is an object of terror. To him one of our own poets has said in solemn invocation, —

> "Come to the bridal chamber, Death;
> Come to the mother, when she feels,
> For the first time, her firstborn's breath;
> Come when the blessed seals
> That close the pestilence are broke,
> And crowded cities wail its stroke;
> Come in consumption's ghastly form,
> The earthquake-shock, the ocean's storm;
> Come when the heart beats high and warm,
> With banquet song, and dance, and wine;
> And thou art terrible, — the tear,
> The groan, the knell, the pall, the bier;
> And all we know, or dream, or fear
> Of agony, are thine."

But it is not of this phantom king that I now speak. Compared with the real death, this may be and often is a delivering angel, whether he comes in the evening, or at midnight, or at cock-crowing, or in the morning, — an angel of deliverance to those who, when he cometh, are found watching. But the death of which I speak is the dying of the soul, the decay of its faculties, the wasting of its powers, the languishing of its strength, — the progressive, unending dying of an immortal soul, with all its unending anguish of unsatisfied longing, unfulfilled desire, baffled hope, pitiless remorse, remediless despair. This is the dread reality at which men ought to tremble. It is no chimera of imagination; it is no spectre of the future, — it is a present reality. It is doing its ghastly work even now in every soul where sin reigns. For the soul that sins is dying. The wages of sin is death.

How sweet, then, is the sound of the gospel to us sinners! How precious is this word of life which tells us that a fountain is opened in the house of David for sin and uncleanness; that there is One who is called Jesus, because He saves His people from their sins; "that if any man sin, we have an Advocate with the Father, Jesus Christ the righteous: and he is the Propitiation for our sins"!

SERMON IV.

REDEMPTION.[1]

And thou shalt call his name Jesus: for he shall save his people from their sins. — ST. MATT. i. 21.

THE signification of the name of the great Redeemer, whose human birth we are soon to commemorate, is here very accurately given: and we naturally look to this definition for its deepest import and profoundest meaning; for it was thus defined before his birth by an angelic messenger from another world. The name itself was not uncommon among the Jews. Under its Hebrew form of Joshua it had been famous in the annals of priestly and patriotic renown; and in its etymological signification of "Saviour," or "help from God," the oppressed sons of Jacob had more than once seemed to hear the note of Israel's deliverance. And as Joshua the son of Nun had been the great standard-bearer of God's people, and in his name had smitten the heathen hip and thigh, so again and again did Israel's fond mothers give this name to their sons in the hope that each son so honored would be the deliverer of his race. But when the true deliverer came, though the

[1] Preached in St. Paul's Church, Detroit, on the morning of the third Sunday in Advent, 1884.

same old name of hope and power was given to him, it was given with a new signification. He was to be his people's Saviour indeed, but it was to be from no mere external evil or external bondage. His great work was to be far more intensive, far more inclusive, far more comprehensive. He was to save them from that which is the secret and source of all real evil and all real bondage: from the deadly disease that was feeding at humanity's heart and preying on its life; from the ghastly brood of ills which that disorder, with woful fecundity, was daily and hourly bringing forth to deal destruction throughout the world, — He was " to save his people from their sins."

If my time permitted me to take a historical view of my subject, I might well speak of the desperate need which was dimly felt for some Saviour and Restorer in the age when Jesus was born. The whole world was lying in inconceivable wickedness and wretchedness. Political servitude and servile bondage, enforced by remorseless Roman legionaries against the brilliant but despairing efforts of such patriots as Ariovistus and the Maccabees, were among the very least of their evils. The expiring forces of paganism had left the Gentile world without hope and without any worthy ideals. Under the degenerating influence of sin and worldliness all the barriers that had guarded society had broken down. By the secret and open assaults of guilty passion the institution of the family had been overthrown. Marriage, which God by an eternal law had declared to be indissoluble except by death, was made a mere abstract of convenience; and divorce, that Nemesis of libertinism, began to desolate the homes of men. Fatherhood was no longer a source of pride; maternity was avoided or prevented as an evil. Parents no longer loved their children, and children no longer honored their parents. The heartless cruelty of the Roman matron who drove her chariot wheels over her father's dead body was only a symptom of the utter debasement into which society had fallen. Now, in the midst of it all, the weariness of hopelessness and despair had settled down like a pall upon the world. Men, women, and children madly flung the gift of life away. It was easier to find men for the bloody games of the amphitheatre than it was to get beasts to fight with them; and so in mere wantonness they hurled themselves against each other's spears, amid the frenzied shouts of a light-minded mob, who, lacking all else that they could delight in, gloated over the brutal spectacle of the arena; or, lacking all else that they could do homage to, lifted up their voices in loud acclaim to salute the monster who happened at the time to wear the imperial purple; and who, in the historian's dreadful phrase, was "at once a priest, an atheist, and a god." Words would fail, however, as time fails, to tell the woe which, after four thousand years of guilt and wrong, had settled down upon the lives of men, when in a vision of the night the unearthly voice of an angel told to a perplexed dreamer in Galilee the coming of the world's Saviour; but it was in a character not looked for, not expected, not desired: He came to save His people from their sins.

It is not necessary, however, to recur to the state of the world at the time of Christ's coming, to understand man's need of deliverance. Sin is an ever-present evil. We have but to study the human heart as it is, to see how great its need, how dire its extremity. We have already learned what sin is, — the fell disorder which scatters evil through man's whole nature, whose work is decrepitude and misery, whose wages is death. From this state no human agency can deliver man; no power can rescue him but a power from above, which comes from beyond the reach of sin's deadly action; for all human powers and faculties are disabled and degenerated under the influence of the universal curse which his sin has inflicted on the race. Let us think for a moment now of the powerlessness and hopelessness of man under the dominion of sin. Laying aside all technical language, let us consider how helpless he is to escape by any agency of his own from the power of evil.

And first, there is a common delusion that sin is like some diseases that are said to run their course and then cease; that is, if sin be left alone it will exhaust itself, and leave the soul but little if any the worse. How common this notion is I need not say. In all ages this has been the delusion of youth, and it often deepens and darkens with advancing years. Who that has been rescued from the glamour of the world does not shudder at the complacency with which the young go forth "to sow their wild oats," as the phrase is; at the confidence with which they leave the father's roof and a mother's care, to go and mingle with the world and learn its ways and its so-called wisdom? Yes; to see the prodigal go forth is a heart-breaking sight to those who know of his peril. Sometimes, indeed, he returns, through God's mercy, but never the same. The substance — the soul's substance — is sure to be wasted, the gladness departed, the joy gone. But often the prodigal never returns at all, but abides in some far country, and sinks into deeper and deeper degradation. And so he confirms the old, old truth, that "whatsoever a man soweth that shall he also reap;" that "he that soweth to the flesh shall of the flesh reap corruption." For oh, one of the worst things about sin is its persistency! In the world around us, as is well known, there is a law called the law of degeneration. When by dint of culture and care some species of animals or plants are domesticated and improved, if they then be released from care and abandoned to their own instincts, they degenerate or revert to the lower type from which they sprung. Thus the trained courser, when turned out, soon becomes the common and shaggy wild horse of the plains; the tumbler pigeon, the winged and crested pigeon of glorious plumage, the carrier dove, degenerate into the wild pigeon of the forest; and the most beautiful roses, when abandoned in a desolate and weed-grown garden, become like the wild roses that blossom in the woods. So throughout all Nature we find a common law of degeneration. But far worse is the degeneration that sin works in the soul. All the baser passions and powers grow stronger and stronger by use, and all the nobler faculties and powers grow weaker and weaker by disuse, until these last are exterminated or disabled, and the man has become mere flesh. Therefore it is that the more sin is indulged, the more hopeless, the more remediless, humanly speaking, it becomes. It has no reactionary, resilient force. Of itself it cannot stop short of death. It may and often does change its form as years roll on. The frivolous, undutiful, pleasure-loving sin of youth often changes into some other form of selfishness, such as avarice, or sensuality, or drunkenness. The thoughtless, lawless, selfish boy may become the grasping or cruel or sensual man; may become by means of his own selfishness what the world calls prudent and prosperous; but in this his sin has not in the least diminished or run its course; it has only deepened and taken on a deadlier form, — deadlier because it is now intrenched behind a cold and inaccessible barrier of selfish thrift and heartless prosperity.

And if sin has no healing power in itself, no more can penalty save and deliver from it, — neither the suffering of present penalty nor the threatening of future punishment. Sin has its present penalty. With all its early glamour, and with all its later delusion and observation, every soul that sins suffers penalty and loss. From the moment that the fell enchantment of the world works its spell upon the soul, it is deluded and deceived, — never rewarded, never appeased, never satisfied. And not only is there discontent and restlessness, unsatisfied longing, consuming desire, the sense of dishonor and failure within the soul, but there is often the external penalty that waits upon transgression. But in none of these is there any remedial power. In all the round of human wretchedness there is no sadder spectacle than to see the soul sorrow and agonize and sicken under the penalty of sin, and at the same time grow harder and more desperate in its sin. And yet it is a common sight. There is a difference, not in degree, but in kind, between the godly sorrow that leadeth to repentance not to be repented of, and the sorrow of the world that worketh death. And this is the profound lesson that it teaches, — that punishment alone cannot reform; that penalty alone has no power to heal the sickness of the soul. Statesmanship is at last beginning to take note of this disheartening truth. If penalty is the only force that is brought to bear upon the criminal, as it too often is, then his last state is sure to be worse than the first. It is now well known that discharged convicts are as a rule our worst criminals. It is by no means uncommon for the thief or burglar who has served out his sentence, to hasten from the very prison doors to the commission of another and a worse crime. Therefore there are thoughtful men in whose estimation our prison system as a remedial system is a total failure; and who believe that as things are, our jails and prisons are but seminaries of crime from which a great and growing criminal class is being constantly officered and recruited. Nay, there are those who believe that for a capital offence it is better and more merciful to hang a man than to send him to prison; for if he go to prison he is almost sure to get worse instead of better, but if he be hanged he may at any rate save his soul. I do not intend, however, to discuss this subject now. Enough has been said to suggest what is confirmed by all observation and experience, — that punishment alone has no power to reform; that penalty cannot save from sin and death.

So as we pass in review all the plans and methods of human reform, we find that there is nothing that man of himself can do in which he can find deliverance from his evil state. And when we add to this state of helplessness the sense of guilty desert which every sinner feels in his heart with reference to a pure and holy God, which drives him away from God, and which necessarily separates him from God, we see how hopeless his natural condition is. And man's despairing efforts have only confirmed this; in all ages, in every clime, beneath every sky, he has sought deliverance from his evil case. Beside lurid altar fires, in the smoke of sacrifice, in the depths of forest, in mountain caves, on hoary heights, beneath academic groves, by meditation, by self-inflicted torture, in philosophy, in religious nescience, in fanaticism, in idolatry, in all the movements and progress and decay of human thought and human effort, man has sought, and has sought in vain for some remedy for the grievous hurt of his soul; for some healer and deliverer from his deadly evil. Many pretenders indeed have appeared, but none have even guessed the true secret of the disorder. Some have proposed external and legislative remedies; some have offered military force or socialistic organization; some have pointed men to the secret chamber of philosophy or to the desert of asceticism. But all have failed, utterly, drearily, disastrously. One there was, however, who came in different guise and with far profounder purpose; who came to heal men and so restore the soul from its dread disorder; and that was He whose name was first breathed by the angel of the annunciation, and was first defined in all the fulness of its meaning by the angel of Joseph's dream: "Thou shalt call his name Jesus; for he shall save his people from their sins."

What man, therefore, was unable to do for himself, the pitiful, merciful God undertook to do for him, and in a manner the most effective, the most wonderful. In the fulness of time He Himself came forth, in the person of the Son, "made of a woman, made under the law, . . . that we might receive the adoption of sons." It is a pious opinion entertained by many divines and sages that the incarnation would have taken place even if man had not sinned and fallen; that it was part of the Divine purpose toward men that at the proper time the great archetype according to which man had been fashioned at creation should be revealed in the Incarnate Word, as the standard and measure of what man made in God's image ought to become. Be this as it may, it was not till man's sin and fall that the hope of deliverance was given in the beautiful promise that Eve, the sorrowing mother of transgression, should also be the mother of salvation. Poor, penitent Eve! deep down in her sorrowing womanly heart the blessed hope was planted, and when her firstborn son came into the world, she fondly thought he might be the deliverer; and so she said, "I've gotten a man from the Lord." What heartbreak came to her, how did the iron enter into her mother-heart, when that son, a fugitive from the face of man, fled away with the blood of his brother on his soul! So did mother after mother cherish in her heart the fond hope that hers should be the seed that should bruise the serpent's head. But ages passed by, — ages of sin and suffering and wrong, — and all hopes were baffled, all expectation denied, until the hours of time's fulness came. Then in a manner ineffable, mysterious, wonderful, the power of the Highest came upon a virgin in the house of David. He in whose image man had been made became a man. In indissoluble union the Godhead and the manhood became one. In majesty and in humility the creating God and the archetypal man appeared in God-manhood. Prophecy had dimly foreseen Him and had hailed Him afar off. It had given Him many names and titles of honor and of power; but when He came, He came wearing the old title of Saviour, bearing the old name of Jehoshua, Joshua, Jesus. But in Him it had a new signification, and was destined to win a new glory; for it meant that He was to save His people from their sins.

Let us think then of Jesus this morning as a Saviour, and of His redemption as salvation from sin. Let us think of all that He was and of all that He did, and of His work and life as a whole. In three respects man's state because of sin was desperate, and, humanly speaking, remediless; that is to say, in respect of his *ignorance*, his *guilt*, his *weakness*. To these Jesus came to apply the appropriate remedy; namely, *truth*, *atonement*, *grace*. And first, one part of His work of salvation He wrought by the revelation which He was, and which He made of the true meaning of time and of the world, of man, of eternity, of God. If we consider the incarnate life of the Son of God as a theophany and a revealing, we see at once what power it had, and still has, to rescue man from the blind error which is a part of sin. In Jesus, man sees God as He is. And wakened by this vision He sees time and the world as they really are. The false theories of life on which sin proceeds are all contradicted in Him. Every falsehood which the world's enchantment tells, every delusion which it weaves with its Circean spell, finds its refutation in Him. Part of the power of sin lies in its specious delusions. Among these delusions is the lie that the world is all; the lie that sensual pleasure is good, that passion is strong, that pride is majestic, that disobedience is wise. Behold how Jesus came and refuted all these immemorial lies. He came in meekness, humility, obedience, renouncing self, and force, and pride, and the world; and doing this He acted the God. Ah, what a lesson it was that He taught, namely, that God is meek: therefore to be meek is to be godlike and great; that God is gentle and loving and merciful: therefore it is great and godlike to be merciful and loving and gentle. And He taught that this world is not all, but is only a fleeting shadow; that the true world is the unseen world where God is and the angels are; and that it is only by renouncing this world that its real good is to be had and the real world is to be won. And then He reintroduced the mighty principle into the world, the golden clew which man had lost and could not find, the majestic secret of the Divine government itself; and that was the principle of self-sacrifice, the principle of the cross, by which He overcame the world. In all, then, that He did, and in all that He taught, in all that He was and suffered and has become, in the majesty of His unequalled wisdom and influence, this is the sum of what He taught. He taught what God is, and what man was intended to be. And doing this He showed the shame, the falseness, the enormity of sin. He showed the grandeur of meekness, the majesty of humility, the strength of obedience, the power of self-sacrifice, the glory of love. Doing this He showed that He was the wisdom and the power of God. Beneath the illuminating splendor of that teaching all the falsehoods of sin and worldliness are exposed. A radiance from another world breaks through upon the life of man. To the eye of faith the unseen things are seen to be the great things, and eternal life to be the real life; and the soul's dignity and peace are the only concern that is worthy of a man, compared with which the whole world is as nothing. For "What shall it profit a man if he shall gain the whole world and lose his own soul?"

But it is not ignorance alone that keeps the soul back from its own destiny, and constitutes the power of sin. No doubt ignorance, obscuration, the blotting out of the higher truths, the dimming of man's spiritual vision, are among the worst effects of sin; and the clearing of the vision, the removing of the cloud of ignorance, constitutes a noble part of Christ's redemption. But this is not all. Not only ignorance, but guilt, stands like a barrier between the sinner and God. And this guilt is not only regarded by Divine justice, but also by human apprehension. The sense of guilty desert, of amenability to condemnation, the guilty sense of demerit and unworthiness, operates to drive the soul from God. No matter how clear the persuasion of those great truths which Christ revealed; no matter how deep the conviction of sin and of its helplessness. Nay, all the more because of the vision of glory, and the consequent sense of sin's enormity, does the sense of guilty desert drive the sinner from God. There is need, then, of atonement, of satisfaction. Not only does God's holiness demand it (and of that I am not speaking now), but man's guilty fear calls out for it. The soul must feel that its guilty desert is taken away. And herein no shame, no artificial pretence of reconciliation, will suffice. The guilty soul will venture upon nothing less than a full, perfect, and sufficient oblation and satisfaction. Ah, long and wearily has man prosecuted his solemn quest for some adequate expiation for his guilt! In bloody rites, in human holocaust, in grim and awful sacrifices, and still in costly ceremonials and ascetic observances; but all in vain. Peace can nowhere be found in all the world but at the foot of the cross, and in the vision of the Lamb that was slain to take away the sins of the world. By faith the sinner sees that that sacrifice was made for him; by faith he appropriates and makes it his own; by faith he wears the marks of it in his daily life. And so his guilty fear is banished. He feels that satisfaction is made. The spirit of bondage is banished by the spirit of adoption, whereby he cries, Abba, Father. Being justified by faith, he has peace with God.

But even this is not enough. Not only is there ignorance or error, and guilt, but infirmity. Man needs not only truth and peace; he needs grace, help from another world, power from on high. And this too is purchased and provided for in Christ's redemption. We have seen, indeed, how the whole effect of His work and life has been to give man health, in revealing the truth, in bringing life and immortality to light, in taking our guilt away. But He has done more. He has organized the means of grace in the faithful use of which His people get life and healing from him; and above all He has sent the Holy Spirit, — the life-giving spirit that reawakens the principle of life in the soul; the spirit of truth to guide us into all truth; the spirit which convicts of sin, which moves to repentance, which awakens faith whereby we appropriate salvation, which "helpeth our infirmities," which gives us joy and peace in believing, which bears witness with our spirit that we are the children of God.

Then, let us sum up all. Sin is darkness: Jesus is light. Sin is guilt: Jesus is peace. Sin is weakness: Jesus is strength. Faith appropriates Him. Conscience chooses Him. Love claims Him. He is our Saviour. He saves us from our sins.

SERMON V.

ETERNAL LIFE.[1]

Verily, verily, I say unto you, He that heareth my word, and believeth on him that sent me, hath everlasting life, and shall not come into condemnation; but is passed from death unto life. — ST. JOHN v. 24.

IN the minds of many thoughtful and devout people, a confused and mistaken notion exists in regard to the terms "eternal life" and "eternal death," and the application of these terms to the soul. The physical catastrophe which we call death is so obtrusive and overwhelming a fact that we are apt to suppose that all death is a catastrophe, and that the soul's eternal life is something which does not begin until this earthly life is over. The truth is, that the terms "eternal life" and "eternal death," as applied to the soul, denote states or conditions of existence which are begun here and simply continue forever hereafter. If we study the New Testament Scriptures freshly and intelligently, we find that this is among the palmary truths brought to light by the gospel, — a truth too often neglected, too often overlooked, but one which, when rightly comprehended, is of the

[1] Preached in St. Paul's Church, Detroit, on the morning of the fourth Sunday in Advent, 1884.

greatest dignity and importance. Among the
many passages in the Divine Word which teach
this, the one which I have just read sufficiently indicates its meaning and scope. You will observe
here that everlasting life is a thing which a man is
declared, on certain conditions, to have in this
world; that the death which is its contradictory is
said to be escaped in this world, and in the very
act of passing over into life; and that the condition of escaping the one and having the other is
faith in God through Jesus. "Verily, verily, I say
unto you, He that heareth my word, and believeth
on him that sent me, hath everlasting life, and shall
not come into condemnation; but it passed from
death unto life."

Now, of the state which is here denominated
eternal death I need not speak this morning further
than to repeat that it is a state belonging to the
sinful, unbelieving soul in this world, out of which
it is here declared possible for the soul now and
here to escape. This death of the soul is not a
catastrophe, but a condition or state, and we have
already seen whence it arises and what it is. It is
the degenerating, desolating, deadening effect of
sin upon the soul and all its higher faculties and
powers. In sin, the soul renounces its true dignity
and turns from its true destiny. The powers intended to apprehend, to choose, to love eternal
things, are voluntarily surrendered to the base and
transitory things of time and sense. The baser
passions and propensities of man control his life,
and as a consequence the soul's higher faculties

begin to dwindle, to degenerate, to languish. And this continuous progressive debasement and decay is known by the awful name of eternal death. It begins now, it is set up here in this life; and the dreadful thing about it is that unless the one remedy be faithfully and timely applied it must persist, this dying of the soul, and must go on forever. For we have seen that of itself it never runs its course; that it has no power in itself to recover, to react, or to cease; that there is no healing or restoring power in penalty, in punishment or anguish; that, short of the one remedy, apart from the one Saviour and Restorer, it is altogether remediless, and must get worse and worse, more helpless, more hopeless, more despairing, as long as the immortal soul shall exist, — that is, forever and forever.

Eternal life, on the other hand, is also a state of the soul that begins here. It is simply the soul's true life, — a life the movements of which, as we have already seen, consist in apprehending truth, choosing right, loving good, in the doing of which man's true nature expands into all the dignity and nobility for which God designed him when He made him in His own image and after His own likeness. In the text we are told that this mighty inward movement of the soul whereby it appropriates salvation and grace is faith in God through Jesus. Here, then, is the great truth of the gospel, — the Son of God has purchased redemption for us. His great and holy name is justified in all the fulness of its divine meaning, in that He lived and died and rose again, and now lives to save His people from their sins; and by faith we appropriate what He has done, and pass from death to life. And let no one suppose that this in itself is a light matter or a small thing. It is the soul's triumph over all that is unworthy and base. "This is the victory that overcometh the world, even our faith." The revelation made by Jesus was of truths that were absolutely undiscoverable by man. It was not that they were mysterious, or complex, or transcendental, but they were so contradictory to the pride and self-sufficiency of the sinful heart. All the imaginations of man's confused and perverted mind were overthrown and set at nought. The strange humility in which He came and acted the God; the meekness in which He showed Divine things and the Divine power to men; the marvellous renunciation of the world and of self; the deep and tender lessons of love which He exemplified and taught; and finally, the strange, unearthly lesson of the cross, the path of absolute self-sacrifice which He trod, and in which He bade his disciples to follow Him as the only road from earth to the skies, — these were lessons and these were truths the living apprehension and the living appropriation of which do constitute the soul's victory over the world, in which the soul does pass from death to life. I need not enlarge upon the heroic character of this achievement. I need not dwell upon the unwelcomeness of such a plan of salvation to the human heart. Just as of old, the turning to Christ means turning away from the world; the choosing of Christ means the renunciation of the world;

belief in God means an awakening to a sense of the vanity and unworthiness of the world, and the transfer of the affections from the phenomenal to the real, from the seen to the unseen, from the vain and transitory to the abiding and eternal. And this is not less difficult now than it has ever been since the world's enchantment first cast its spell upon the soul of man. The glamour of sense is not less fascinating now than when in olden days the siren voices of Circe's nymphs floated over dancing waves to lure the strong Ulysses and his wandering companions to their ruin. Nay, it is all the more seductive and dangerous now, because it comes to us, to so many of us, in the sober guise of worldly business or society, of worldly thrift, of worldly care, of worldly prudence. But if with true strength and constancy of soul we refuse to be betrayed into a forgetfulness of our birthright; if in the midst of all worldly pleasures and worldly cares we insist that our souls shall live their true life; if amid the din and roar of this world's busy pursuits we bend the ear of the spirit to catch the Divine Word, and with living faith believe not in time and the world only, but in eternity and God, then shall eternal life abide in us. For "he that heareth my word and believeth on him that sent me hath everlasting life, and shall not come into condemnation; but is passed from death unto life."

Now, what I wish to do to-day, is to point out to you the dignity and the joy of this true life of the soul, this everlasting life of faith; and if we can know the secret of its blessedness here, we shall know what its blessedness shall be hereafter. For the redeemed and ransomed soul simply lives on from this world into the next; and the blessedness, the gladness, the joy that it has here, it shall have the same in kind, though in larger measure, forever hereafter.

And first, to the justified soul there is the joy of living its true life. The soul has its proper life; and in the very living of it freely, without the confusion and discord of sin, there is deep and ineffable gladness. We look around us and see the joyousness of all undiseased, unfettered, and undisturbed life. All living creatures seem to exult, and often to break out in transports of joy, in the very act and sense of living. With verdure clad, and in light arrayed, the fields and hillsides afford a scene on which the flocks and herds disport themselves in spring, while from the leafy choirs of overhanging woods the birds pour forth exultant strains of song, and even the flowers, the beautiful flowers, seem to smile with gladness, as if it were a very joy to be beautiful and to live. You all remember the beautiful little idyl of Wordsworth, whose great poetic soul was always so profoundly stirred at the sight of Nature's beauty and life. He said: —

> " I wandered lonely as a cloud
>   That floats on high o'er vales and hills,
> When all at once I saw a cloud,
>   A host of golden daffodils,
> Beside the lake, beneath the trees,
> Fluttering and dancing in the breeze.

"Continuous as the stars that shine
  And twinkle on the Milky Way,
They stretched in never ending line
  Along the margin of a bay:
Ten thousand saw I at a glance,
Tossing their heads in sprightly dance.

"The waves beside them danced, but they
  Outdid the sparkling waves in glee:
A poet could not but be gay
  In such a jocund company.
I gazed and gazed, but little thought
What wealth the show to me had brought.

"For oft when on my couch I lie
  In vacant or in pensive mood,
They flash upon that inward eye
  Which is the bliss of solitude,
And then my heart with pleasure fills,
And dances with the daffodils."

So in all life there is joy; much more in the soul's true life. In the free exercise of its noblest faculties; in the free use of its noblest powers; in the free apprehension of Divine truth, the free choosing of the right, the unselfish loving of the beautiful and the good, — it is a joy even now and here so to live the true life of the soul. And when we come to analyze this joy, we find that in all its details it is a life of blessedness. For, first, there is the joy of triumph, the *gaudium certaminis*, that courts and enjoys the well-won victory. For as all life is a conflict and a victory over whatsoever hinders or attacks it, much more is the soul's true life a continual conflict and victory. Sense, with all its delusions and new sorceries, interposes to obscure or terminate the soul's lofty vision of far-off truth. Evil, with all its seductive wiles, attempts to betray the soul to sin and wrong. Worldly and carnal pleasures woo the soul's affections from their true and worthy objects. To resist these is conflict worthy of heroic souls; to stand steadfast, to be true to truth, goodness, to righteousness, — this is victory, and the joy of it is bliss to the struggling, conquering soul. And when the soul's victorious inner life is translated into worthy outward action, that outward life becomes heroic too, — the life of a knightly soul that proves its knighthood and receives its reward in scattering error, in righting wrong, in helping the weak, in relieving the oppressed, and in doing his duty to God and all the world.

And then there is the joy of progress. For the soul's true life is a progress from the less to the greater, from the partial to the more perfect good. At first its movements are feeble, its apprehensions of truth are dim and confused; the motions of its moral nature are indistinct; the play of its spiritual affections is unsteady. But as the soul's life advances, all these nobler functions are better discharged, all its nobler faculties grow stronger. Temptations that were once mighty become powerless; sins that were once easy become impossible. The spell of worldliness is broken; the soul expands to the measure of the stature of a man in Christ Jesus. There is growth in humility, and so there is no more galling and fretting of pride.

There is growth in meekness, and so the burden of resentment is laid aside. There is growth in faith, and so the unseen things are seen with more and more distinctness to be the great thing. There is growth in hope, and so the soul grows glad and young as it lays hold on the hope of eternal life. There is growth in love, — in the blissful love that never faileth, that suffereth long and is kind, that is not easily provoked, thinketh no evil; that beareth all things, believeth all things, hopeth all things, endureth all things.

And then there is the joy of self-sacrifice. Self-sacrifice for duty and for love is the very joy of the soul's true life. Here, now, is a great and recondite truth. Man had forgotten it. With all his thinking he could not rediscover it; with all his searching he could not find it out. But God revealed it in Jesus. And revealing it He showed not only the Divine wisdom and power, but also the Divine blessedness. In his selfishness man had tried all other kinds of sacrifice in his quest for some kind of offering that his soul might delight in. For he dimly knew that somehow, not in getting merely, but in giving, his soul's true wealth must consist. So he lavished wildly of all his costliest and best. In Oriental splendor, in Greek beauty, in Roman pageantry, in barbaric pomp and magnificence, he prosecuted his despairing quest for some way to get the hidden bliss that belongs to loving, when suddenly the cross of Jesus flashed the Divine truth upon the weary world. In self-sacrifice love finds its bliss, its hidden joy, its secret gladness. It is a lesson for heroic souls, and the world with characteristic cowardice shrinks from it; but even the world is learning at last this great lesson of the cross. When we look around us, we see that selfishness not only works almost all the evil that man inflicts on man, but that selfishness is the great woe of the human heart. Not only does it work the sorrow which the drunkard, the gambler, the thief, the libertine inflict on others, but it makes them what they are, and is always to them the poisoned source of unhappiness and unrest. The selfish man is always the unblest man. No selfish soul is happy. Selfishness always fails of its aim; it always misses its mark. But in loving and dutiful self-sacrifice the soul finds its joy and its exaltation, even as Jesus our great Exemplar, who for the joy that was set before Him endured the cross, despising the shame, and is even set down at the right hand of the Majesty on high. Who does not understand something of this? Who are the great and happy souls of earth? Not those, assuredly, who look for base ease, or sordid gain, or selfish advantage, or guilty pleasure; but the pure and strong and lofty souls, who in loving the unseen and following lofty ideals gladly sacrifice themselves for what they love. The patriot who goes at his country's summons to battle; the father and husband who scorns delight and lives laborious days for wife and children; the mother who turns away from all delights to bend in yearning tenderness above the couch of her sick or afflicted child; the Christian man and woman who in loving, dutiful deeds of brotherly love and good-will delight to help the unfortunate and make the wretched happy, — these are the great and happy souls, and in their self-sacrifice they find the highest joy of their soul's true life.

In a word, then, the soul's true life in this world is the life of faith, hope, and of love. In the victory of its faith, the progress of its hope, the glad self-sacrifice of its love, its joy consists. And oh, dear brethren, compared with this joy, how utterly vain and unsatisfying are all the other joys of earth! For all other joys are outside of man, and cannot reach the centre of his being. Therefore, you may lavish all imaginable splendor and all imaginable wealth upon man, and if he have not the secret joy, this peace of God in his heart, the soul is restless and wretched, and poor and unsatisfied. But with this joy and gladness in the heart, the soul's true life is blissfully, peacefully lived, spite of sorrow, spite of pain, spite of care; nay, it is lived through these, and through the dark valley and shadow of death itself, into the fuller, richer, more abounding life beyond the grave.

And this brings me to my concluding thought. We have seen what the soul's true life in this world is. What shall it be in the next world but the same in kind, though in fuller, larger measure? In an age of curious and adventurous research like this, it is impossible not to feel a profound interest in what, after all, is the great mystery of all mysteries, — the life beyond the grave. As knowledge grows and thought widens, men become more and more intolerant of mystery. For long ages the great river of Egypt flowed out of mystery to the sea. Year by year it rose and fell, overflowing its banks and fertilizing all the plain. Mighty empires rose and flourished along its course. Toiling millions builded the great pyramids to be the monuments of forgotten greatness. Dynasty after dynasty ruled and passed away. The great Sphinx, with mournful visage, saw them come and go, and still the great river rose and fell, and no man knew and no man guessed the secret of its annual inundation. But this age could not longer brook the great secret that lay concealed in the heart of the dark continent. Traveller after traveller, adventurer after adventurer, set out to discover the source of the Nile, and so to solve the mystery. With increasing eagerness and in larger number the men pressed forward. Many went, but few returned, until at last the secret was discovered. So also into the mystery that broods in icy desolation over the Polar Seas. Men have gone and perished, and still have gone, and are ready still to go, to find the secrets of that wild waste whose icy barriers have hitherto defied the adventurous efforts of man. Still more do men long to know something of that undiscovered country from whose bourn no traveller returns. Into its darkness all the generations of men have hitherto journeyed, with trembling steps and slow, *sed nulla vestigia retrorsam*. Who, then, shall tell us of it? Who shall disclose the majestic secrets of the future life of the soul? We look in vain to speculative philosophy. Some splendid guesses it has made, but only guesses. We turn to Revelation; but at first glance it seems to be strangely mute, as if it knew not, or had no message to tell. True, Lazarus once came back after four days and nights in the other world; but we have no record that he ever told of the things that he heard and saw. And a greater than Lazarus, to whom that world was always open, before whose vision it was always outstretched, whose spirit was always bathed in its supernal glory, who passed as a visitant into that world through the gate of death, and then returned and companied forty days with His disciples, — even He has seemed to tell us nothing. Why is it? May it not be because there was very little to tell, except what we may know already? We know that the life of that other state of the soul's true life, the life eternal, begins here. We know what it is here. We know in what its joy and its everlasting nobleness and dignity consist here, — in the victory of faith, in the progress and aspiration of hope, in the joy of self-sacrificing love. Must not these continue to be the sources of its blessedness hereafter? The only difference shall be that the limitations of sin, the hindrances of earthliness, shall be removed. Unfettered and free, the soul shall expand in the perpetual delight of life and love and peace, — the delight of growing knowledge, the delight of more and more adequate utterance, the security and peace of more perfect self-consecration, the deep and tender joy of more entire self-sacrifice. How this shall be, I cannot tell.

Nor do I care to hear of elysian fields and sunny slopes, of celestial towers and golden streets. The imagery with which prophets and seers have pictured that world and its employments may be reality or metaphor. For one, I do not care to know. It is enough for me to know this one thing, — that the soul's true life, the eternal life, begun here, shall continue after death substantially the same, and that its joys shall be the same, only fuller, larger, richer. Oh, then, let me ask myself this question: Am I living now the soul's true life, — the everlasting life of faith and hope and love, — and am I finding now and here the joy and the blessedness of that life? If not, then even heaven itself would be a hell to my untutored soul. But if I do know the joy and peace of believing, then eternal life is mine already.

SERMON VI.

THE SIGNS OF THE TIMES.[1]

The Pharisees also with the Sadducees came, and tempting desired him that he would show them a sign from heaven. He answered and said unto them, When it is evening, ye say, It will be fair weather: for the sky is red. And in the morning, It will be foul weather to-day: for the sky is red and lowering. O ye hypocrites, ye can discern the face of the sky; but can ye not discern the signs of the times? — ST. MATT. xvi. 1–3.

IT was characteristic of the religion of Jesus Christ, that among all the religions which have solicited the consent of mankind, it was the first to refuse to appeal to the lying wonders which superstition craved; that from the first it refused to rest its claims to acceptance on portent or even on miracle merely; but it rested them rather on the truth which it proclaimed, and the fitness of that truth to the need of the world. When at cultured Athens or warlike Sparta an enterprise requiring conduct or valor was meditated, it was the custom to send a messenger across plain and mountain to Delphi, to hear from the lips of the Priestess of Apollo the mystic words which might tell of its success or failure. When a conquest was projected at ancient Rome, after the legions were mustered and the

[1] Preached in Christ Church, Detroit, on the morning of the first Sunday in Advent, 1885.

plans were laid, it was customary to send an augur to some neighboring height, to watch the portents of the sky and read the omens of the hour; and if the flight of birds were auspicious, or Jove thundered from the left, or other favorable augury appeared, then and then only did the embattled legions dare to take up the line of march to the enemy's country. But the Christian soldier, though he too would fain know something of the coming time, may well disdain all the superstitions of divination, even as his great Leader disdained them. Jesus laid down the only principle of genuine prognostication, the only principle of scientific augury, when He bade men study the signs of the times in their attempts to forecast the future. For the evening foretells the morning, and the morning leads on the day. All the hours are linked together, and each as it takes its flight ushers in a kindred hour. Therefore it is that " thro' the ages one increasing purpose runs; " and we must read the signs of the times that now are, if we would guess what the future of the world is to be.

In this series of Advent Sermons I desire to speak of the work which lies before the Church of Christ in this land and age. In doing this, though I must speak without reserve of hindrances as well as of helps, of portents of evil as well as portents of good, yet I stand here as one who looks for victory, for I believe in the coming triumph of our Lord. All around us there are, I believe, the signs of the coming of His power; but because those signs abound, it behooves us to set our house in order; to reform whatsoever is amiss in our own economies and the working of them; to sound the call to duty throughout all our borders; to cast away the works of darkness and put upon us the armor of light, because our salvation is nearer than when we believed. In this first sermon, therefore, I shall briefly and rapidly discourse on the great and beneficent career which Anglo-Saxon Christianity ought to accomplish in this land and age, and of the personal effort and consecration which we ought to yield in its service. Then in the following sermons I shall speak of the function and mission of the same Christianity, and of the evils that it ought to correct in our domestic, our business, our social life.

Let me then in the briefest and simplest way speak of the general course which Christian activity and beneficence may be reasonably expected to take in this land, if we are faithful. To do this in an oracular way would of course be rash and presumptuous; but to be an observer of contemporary facts and tendencies, and to try to interpret the meaning of them, is something, surely, which can be undertaken by the humblest and most self-distrustful. The problem of the future of Christianity in this land is to be worked out by factors that are in operation now; and the character and operation of those factors are among the signs of the times which we can discern and interrogate if we will. Among those factors some are constant and unchanging; as, for instance, the ever-present evil of sin, the undiminishing corruption of unregenerate human nature, the ceaseless activity of the Spirit of grace, and the inexhaustible efficacy of the old gospel of love and power. God's revelation of His will, moreover, in His written Word and in His Church's fixed faith and unchanging order, are among the constant factors which we may count on in our effort to read the problem of the future. Other factors are to be found in the operation of certain great economical, ethnological, political laws which are now at work, and which establish a certain stream of tendency or current of wants which we may estimate with more or less accuracy. And last of all, there are the factors of personal effort, personal faithfulness, personal devotion, which, while they are the most variable of all, are yet those which most entirely depend on ourselves and our children. I will venture, then, to speak this morning of the work of Christianity in this land and age: (1) From a consideration of the people and the civilization in the midst of which it is to be carried forward; (2) From a consideration of the means and agencies with which this Church is equipped for carrying it on; and (3) From a consideration of the personal effort and personal devotion which we are called to apply to it.

First, then, of the people and the civilization of this great country. It is customary to say that our people are now, and must continue to be, a composite people, made up of elements so various that as a whole our people must differ materially from every other people on the face of the globe.

And, indeed, when we study our history, and the statistics of emigration to this land, we find that the Keltic, the Saxon, the Teutonic, the Scandinavian, the Latin races have all come hither in large though unequal numbers, bringing their own characteristics and traditions with them, and that here they have freely mingled together under the protection of equal laws. From this it might be expected that the resulting race would be a new people altogether, differing from all others as the *tertium quid* of the chemist is unlike the simples of which it is compounded. And yet when we come to look at the people of this land, we find as a matter of fact that there is no such variation from the original type on which all these varieties have been grafted as one would suppose. With such slight differences as are to be accounted for on other grounds, the American people continue to be a branch of the great English race, keeping the ideal English type, English minded and English hearted, re-enacting the laws of Alfred, and speaking the language of Shakspeare and Milton.

Now, the fact that the people of this land have continued unwaveringly and persistently to be English in civilization, in spite of the enormous dilution by emigration that has been going on for a hundred years, is a fact of immense significance. Millions of other races have come hither,— Kelts, Latins, Scandinavians, Slavs,— but they have not been able in the slightest degree to vary our civilization from its English type and character. It was but a handful of Englishmen that came to Virginia, New England, New York, Pennsylvania, the Carolinas, Georgia; and yet they so impressed their ethnical type upon this nation that they have made it Anglican forever. The reasons for this are significant and instructive. There is not time to consider them here. Suffice it to say that the fact is by no means isolated or accidental. From the first, that race of Anglo-landers and their congeners who came from the banks of the Zuyder Zee have been so persistent that they have refused to part with any of their characteristics as they have mingled with other races. Wherever they have gone, they have given their civilization to all with whom they have mingled. You will find a survival of the old Anglo-Saxon hundred in the New England town-meeting and in the Michigan town-meeting; and you will find trial by jury, and the *habeas corpus*, and the English school, and the English home, — even as you find everywhere the English language and English laws. These institutions endure, and they in turn help to mould all comers to the one type of free manhood in this free land. Alien races that come hither are emancipated of their race peculiarities. In our free atmosphere, beneath our open sky, their children are made over, as it were, and transformed into American citizens; and as a result we soon see them speaking the English language, reading English Bibles, living in English homes. I have not the time now to speak of this as I would. All I can now say is that this mighty people, though a composite people as to its elements, is, and shall forever be, homogeneous in its character; and that whatsoever form of religion is best suited to the needs and idiosyncrasies of the English-speaking races is the religion which is charged with the great, the awful responsibility of shaping their social and religious destiny.

Now, I am sure you will acquit me of the shallow presumption of ecclesiastical pretentiousness in bringing these considerations before you. My simple purpose is that we should realize our opportunities and responsibilities as a Church in this land; for as our opportunities, so are our responsibilities, great and constantly increasing. Believing that great and awful responsibilities rest upon this Church as the historical Church of the Anglo-Saxon race, it must humble and sober us even to recount them; nay, it would doubtless discourage us to face our responsibilities unless at the same time we might lean on the thought that God's providence in history has sent this Church to this land to be our guide in faith and morals, and that He has equipped her with special agencies to do His work among this great people. For in the first place this historic Church, around which all the noblest traditions of Anglo-Saxon Christianity have clustered, supplies to the people of this land the one venerable authority in religion which it is the instinct of our people to long for; for with all their progressiveness, they do cling to what is customary, and venerate what has come down from their own past. This is obvious in manners, customs, laws; as time goes on it will be more and more obvious in religion also. In the next place, her advantage is great in her sober, ethical, undogmatic teaching, free from metaphysical subtlety, free from superstition, mysticism, false enthusiasm, — a religion of manly and womanly activity. One of the most marked peculiarities of this as of all English-speaking races is their intolerance of all mere sentimentalism and mysticism; the devotion of their thought to what is practical. In the long run they refuse to be misled by false enthusiasms, such as make the French doctrinaire, the Latin mystical, the German transcendental, the Irish superstitious. Nothing can long hold the allegiance of their minds and their hearts but what is sober, undogmatic, practical; and this it is which distinguishes the tone and temper of Anglo-Saxon Christianity. Next, it is her advantage and her glory that she is the one Church which has always put duty and conscience to the fore; which in every Sunday morning service, in the reading of God's eternal law, invokes conscience, appeals to conscience, respects conscience, and then leaves conscience free to make and enforce its judgments. This has been the course of the Englishman's love of liberty the wide world over, because liberty has thus been made to him a sacred thing, chastened by the responsibilities of moral freedom; for long before the battle of Trafalgar the English Church flung this signal to the breeze: The Church of England expects every man to do his duty. Lastly, the

Church has the great advantage of having a decent and stately, but at the same time a sober and reasonable, worship. For while this race does love a decent and stately ceremonial, anything that is fantastic, or sham, or unreal, it cannot long tolerate. It is its nature to express less than it feels rather than more. A certain reserve is the habit of its honest self-respect. Above all things it demands manly simplicity and reality; and this it finds to its increasing contentment and spiritual peace in the simple, orderly, real worship of Anglo-Saxon Christianity.

Now, to what do these considerations lead? To the thought, first, of the great responsibility, and then of the lofty dignity, of our calling as Christian men. Compared with the other agencies that are shaping the course and moulding the destiny of this community, of this people, the one agency of most surprising dignity and import is this: In all ages and in all lands man's religious interests are supreme. No matter what sky bends above him, nor in what scenes of beauty or grandeur his lot is cast, the one thought that redeems the world from commonplace is the thought of another. No matter what lofty enterprise engages him, nor what deeds of high emprise his strong right hand finds to do; the one interest that always and everywhere ought to be his chiefest care is the interest that cleaves to his immortality. But here in this busy land, our sober, ethical, practical religion is more to us even than this. It lies at the foundation of our public liberty and national greatness. It sentinels our homes and guards our domestic purity and peace. It hovers over our society, to beat back with guardian wings the foul harpies of evil desire and unbridled passion that would batten on its innocent beauty. It stands an invisible angel even in the hearts of trade, to smile on integrity and uprightness, and to shame fraud and double-dealing away. And this it does, not as an alien religion or foreign cult, but as one that is at home in this free land, and that is in full sympathy with all that is good in our national and social life. Nay, it is the genius of our Anglo-Saxon Christianity that has shaped our civilization and given us our liberty; and in guarding these from all harm she is but watching over her own, even as a mother yearns over her children whom she delights in. What nobler service, then, can men and women engage in than this? Where can you find an interest that makes such an appeal to all that is noble, high-minded, aspiring in man, as this work which is committed to the Churchmen of this land?

What this work is in its domestic, social, business aspect, I am to try hereafter to tell you. Let me conclude now with this single remark: I have briefly recounted some of the signs of the times, some of the omens of success that attend us. Let me not fail to say that there are not wanting some portents of evil in the horoscope of our busy and crowded future. He is blind and worse than blind who does not see vast and minatory dangers gathering thick on the right and on the left and full in front of our path of progress. There are dangers of class combinations, wherein men will forfeit their personality and lose the dignity of their individuality. There are dangers of class conflicts, wherein all that is sacred will be overthrown. There are dangers of materialism with its degrading influence, and of intemperance and passion with their Circean spell, to convert men into swinish brutes. There is a subtle scepticism in the air like a foul malaria, which is imperilling the life of our people, because it bereaves them of their faith in all that is noble; which is sapping the manhood of our men because it obscures their belief in the God in whose image man was made. What now is the duty of the hour but to rally on the standard of our great Captain; for all the redeemed to gather around the altar, and thence, and in the strength there gained, to go forth to do valiantly for the Lord? In times and lands less favored than ours, when the hosts of heathenness raged around the borders, it was then that the plumed and belted knight rode forth to keep the marches, while Christian women hid themselves behind convent walls, to spend their nights in weeping, their days in prayer. But in these better days we have no feudal knighthood, because all our men are called to be knights; and we need no cloistered nuns, because all our women are called to be sisters of mercy, women of prayer. In all our homes there may be saintly women and knightly, godly men. From their portals the one may issue forth as gentle ministers of mercy to the poor, all the better and more Christ-like because no conventual garb marks them to be seen of men; while the other may pass along these streets to do deeds all the more knightly and true because the cross is in their hearts instead of on their shields, and because the weapons of their warfare are not carnal but spiritual. Yes, men and women can live as grandly and die as sweetly and as gloriously to-day as ever they did. And oh, this is what is needed to-day as much as ever, — that men should live, as you and I have known more than one to live, like Bayards and Galahads; and should die as you and I have known them to die, like an Arthur who yielded up a stainless sword, or an Agnes who joyously went to meet the bridegroom as the sun was sinking to his rest at the hour of evening prayer.

SERMON VII.

HOME.[1]

God setteth the solitary in families. — Ps. lxviii. 6.

THERE is a word which is peculiar to our English speech, — so peculiar that it is impossible to translate it accurately into any other language. It may therefore be said that the thing which it signifies is in its strictest sense peculiar to those to whom that speech is the mother tongue; and that word is *Home*. In its larger meaning it may be said that the religion of our Lord Jesus Christ created it. In its best meaning and highest development we believe that it is chiefly to be found among those nations who use the good old word itself; that is, among the English-speaking peoples of the world.

Some words contain a history in themselves, and are the monuments of great movements of thought and life. Such a word is *Home*. With something like a sacramental sacredness it enshrines a deep and precious meaning and a history. That the English-speaking people and their congeners alone should have this word, indicates that there are certain peculiar domestic and social traits of

[1] Preached in Christ Church, Detroit, on the morning of the second Sunday in Advent, 1885.

character belonging to them, of which this word is the monument and sign; and those traits have found their expression in the economy and order of the home. When we study their history we find that from the very first they have been distinguished, as Tacitus tells us, by the manly and womanly virtues of fidelity and chastity; by the faithful devotion of wife to husband and husband to wife; by the recognized headship and guardianship of the married man as indicated in the old word *husband*, and the domestic dignity and function of the married woman as indicated in the old word *wife*, — betokening the presence of those home-making, home-keeping, home-loving qualities of mind and heart which have always belonged to this sturdy race. And when upon these ethnical qualities the vitalizing, sanctifying influence of Christianity was brought to bear, the outcome has been the building up of the noblest of all the institutions of the Christian life. Therefore where the English language is spoken, this word is among the sweetest that human lips can fashion. Therefore where an English civilization is established, this institution enshrines all that is most precious to the human heart. No man is poor, no matter what storms of ill fortune have beaten upon him, who can still find refuge beneath its sacred shelter; and no man is rich, no matter how splendid his fortune or his lot, who cannot claim some spot of earth as his home.

My purpose, however, is neither philological nor ethnological. It is rather to speak to you to-day, in briefest, simplest language, of the function of Christianity in the home. However its economy has been modified by ethnical peculiarities, it is God who has set the solitary in families; or, as the Hebrew may be more accurately translated into our English speech, " He hath set the solitary in the home." It is upon His unspeakable enactment that this great institution rests. Its function is to carry out His purposes in training and ennobling men to do His will. Its perfection is the reflection of His love in the majestic order of His Godhead with fatherhood, sonship, life; its beatitude is the maintenance on earth of the peace and purity of heaven. It is the model after which all the other institutions of our civil society are builded. The true unit of the social and civil structure is the man-woman, the husband and wife made one, dwelling together in unity and loving concord, with the children, the offspring and objects of their love, around them. In their relations with one another each finds his own completeness; and all are hallowed and sanctified by the peace of God, which, if it reigns anywhere on earth, is surely to be found in the Christian home.

Taking the Christian home as we know it, then, there are certain broad features of its economy the mention of which will serve to bring out its character. The first of these is its unity of orderly administration, in the supreme headship of one man, the husband; the supreme dignity of one woman, the wife; the providence of parental love in the nurture of children, and the natural piety of children in their reverence and obedience to their parents. Of course all these rest on monogamous marriage, that holy and ineffable bond which unites the wedded pair, and makes them one, — a bond which is the sacramental sign of a profound and mysterious oneness of soul and spirit, in which each personality is lost in the other, which therefore the Divine Master declared to be indissoluble except by death. Marriage is the fulfilment of a divine law, without which no human being is complete. When God made man male and female, he enacted that each could not be complete without the other. The question which is superior is therefore idle. The one is the complement to the other. Made for one another, each finds completeness only in holy matrimony, which is therefore a noble vocation to which every one is called, and from which no one is entitled to turn away, when no insuperable obstacle is interposed to forbid it. In marriage, then, and its resulting unity, the man is the husband and head, because in him strength, reason, justice abound; the woman is the wife and consort, because in her are to be found the gracious tact, the unerring instinct, the loyalty to love and duty, which are necessary to soften and humanize the strength, reason, justice of the man; while the children are under supreme obligation to obedience and reverence, and are at the same time entitled to nurture, training, and care; for this is not only the honorable office, but it is likewise the highest duty of those who bring children into the world, — that they should not only love them, but also train and equip them for time and for eternity.

With these preliminary observations, let us now briefly consider the Christian home, first with reference to its discipline, then with reference to its education, then with reference to the blessedness that belongs to it, and lastly with reference to the dangers which threaten it.

And first, with reference to the discipline of the home, it is to be remembered that there is a home discipline to which all the members thereof are subject, — the father and mother not less than the children. The husband and father, the wife and mother, while they are the source of authority in the home, are themselves under the authority of the God and Father of all, of whose great economy they are the earthly representatives. The only basis, for instance, upon which the headship of the husband can securely rest, is in its conformity to the headship of Christ over His church. Saint Paul uttered a great and profound truth when he declared marriage to be the earthly homologue of that union in which Christ and His church are joined together; and it is only in following Christ that the true function of the head of the home can be discharged. In Christ the husband sees the model of what he ought to be. From Him he learns that all his true authority is an authority to be derived from self-surrender; that all his real power is power to be derived from self-sacrifice. Wherever you see this principle obeyed by the head of the home, acting not as a brutal tyrant or selfish despot, but as one who because he is strong surrenders himself, and who because he is large-minded, large-hearted, sacrifices himself, there you see a real head of the home, whom all reverence and gladly obey. Oh, if the husbands, the heads of our homes, were only Christ-like men, men who rely not on external authority or external force, but on the authority and power which belong to loving self-sacrifice, believe me, almost all the domestic discord and confusion which so abound would disappear! In this, as in all things, influence, success, greatness, are to be gained and learned at the feet of the great Master, who laid down the rule of all headship and leadership when He said, " Let him that would be greatest do ministry and service; even as the Son of man came not to be ministered unto, but to minister, and to give His life a ransom for many."

Nor is the wife, the husband's consort, exempt from this discipline of self-sacrificing love. Such service, indeed, the fond mother-heart of woman is quick to render, and therein lies the hiding of her power. But this service is due not to children only, but to the husband as well. And this is to be shown not only in those gentle ministries of the home which every good wife is glad to render, and in the rendering of which her true queenship lies, but it is to be shown likewise in the reverence which she ought always to feel toward the husband. It was not for nothing that the apostle, in bidding the husband love and cherish his wife, adds the injunction, "And let the wife see that she reverence her husband." I know, indeed, that there often seems to be little or nothing to reverence; and yet to the true wife there must always be something even in the weakest and most unworthy. Just as the true son always sees something to venerate in his mother, and the true husband always sees something to love in his wife, so does the true wife always see something to reverence in that manhood which God has given to her in her husband. And whensoever the wife acts on this principle she calls out what is noblest in her husband. She helps to make him like a prince, because with loving eyes she looks on him as a prince. She helps to make him like a king, because she expects him to act like a king. Nay, each can help to make the other what each believes the other to be; and as the years roll on they grow more like each other and dearer to each other in the tender bonds of wedded love.

So, likewise, the true basis on which parental authority over children rests, is the great fact of the fatherhood of God. It is only when parents look up and study that Divine fatherhood,—a fatherhood which wills the perfection of the children, and sets them the example of perfectness; a fatherhood that knows how to hear and answer prayer, and to give all good things to those that ask; nay, a fatherhood that knows how to give itself in utter self-sacrifice, the measure of whose love is the cross,—it is only when parents know how to study and catch the spirit of this fatherhood that they know how both to rule and care for their children. To such parental authority I need not say that children ought to be altogether obedient in all things. To such fatherhood and motherhood most children are in glad subjection. But in all cases the duty of the child to be in subjection and to obey in all things lawful is absolute. The true discipline of the home, while tender and loving, should never tolerate disobedience. The rule of the household ought never to be despotic. The utmost care should be exercised never to require what is unreasonable, and not to require too much. But of this the parents must be the judge, and children should be lovingly trained in complete obedience. The characteristic sin of childhood is disobedience, and it includes and leads on to all other sins. But obedience is the crown and grace of childhood, without which no child can learn to be strong and great; without which no child can be lovable or lovely.

These general considerations show plainly what the proper education is that belongs to the Christian home. The Christian home is a school wherein the parents as well as the children learn divine things, not simply or chiefly from any didactic teaching, but from the harmonious working of these relations of headship, fatherhood, motherhood, sonship, all chastened and ennobled by the loving self-sacrifice which pervades the Christian home. There are some aspects of those sublime truths, God's fatherhood, Christ's headship, the wisdom and power of the cross, that never can be learned except as they are disclosed in the experiences of the Christian household. Such truths are not taught didactically, but are learned experimentally,—absorbed, as it were, into the thought and feeling of all its inmates, and made part of their very life. Therefore it is that the home is not only a school but a church. In its sanctuary all the most blessed truths of our holy religion are enshrined, and around the altar of its hearthstone its most benign influence is shed, to fit and train all who gather there, not only for the duties of time, but also for the dignities and labors of eternity. Therefore, so much depends on the religious life of the home,—not merely on its religious teaching, but its religious life,—so much, that if this be right nothing else can be wholly wrong; so much, that if this be wrong nothing else can be altogether right.

In the next place, let me speak just a word, in passing, of the dangers which beset it. I continue to speak of the Christian home. One trembles to think how frail and uncertain the foundation on which the unchristian home must rest. We grieve, but we do not wonder, when such homes, with all their treasures, rush down to hideous ruin. But the Christian home. Let me speak of three only of the dangers which assail it,—care, worldliness, and passion. Just a word of each of these.

And first, of care. The lives of all earnest men are full of care. Perhaps at no time in the world's history has the care of life set more heavily upon the workers and thinkers of the world than it does to-day. Much of this care, no doubt, is fruitless and needless. The remedy for it is the cheerfulness that is born of inward peace. But much of the care of business and of thought is inevitable in this busy age. Men have to toil and struggle to keep their place while the busy world is moving. There is one thing that can be done, however, and that is, we can keep care away from the sacred precincts of the home. When the husband and father enters its portal he should always leave his cares behind him, and mingle with its joys with a light and happy heart. For lack of just this, many a home that would otherwise be happy is dark and desolate. The knitted brow of care will sadden and darken the brightest home. And this is true of the wife as well as the husband. How many Marthas make their home unhappy while they are cumbered with much serving! How many destroy the peace and blessedness of home because they are careful and troubled about many things!

Even more fatal to the peace and safety of the home is worldliness, — the worldliness of the husband which takes him away from his home in the calm evenings, which ought as a rule to be hallowed and sanctified there, to be spent at his counting-room, or at some place of amusement, or at his club. Men who make this the rule of their lives soon abdicate the true headship of their homes; nay, they often break up their homes or desolate them altogether. But even worse is the worldliness of the wife. Why need I speak of it?

Let me rather say this: No woman is fit to be the queen that she ought to be in her own household, who does not, no matter what her station may be, find her chief pleasure and count her chief delight in the employments and endearments of her home.

And lastly, passion. Not to speak of its darker aspects, — the fretful, peevish, irascible, ungovernable temper, the hasty word, the harsh unloving look, the little neglects, the little unkindnesses, — oh, how often do these break up the peace, and finally desolate the home! Therefore there is need of prayer in the home. Therefore there is need that the fire of sacrifice should be always kept burning on its altars. In order to keep these lurking demons, care, worldliness, and passion, from stealing in to work woful mischief there, there is need that the husband should be a man of God, that the wife should be a woman of prayer, and that the children should be trained in the ways and walks of godliness, and be brought up in the nurture and admonition of the Lord.

But when this is so, then we see the blessedness of a Christian home. How shall I try to describe it? With what words shall I attempt to tell of its beatitude? Beneath its shelter alone can the careworn toiler and thinker lay his heavy burden down; in its calm haven alone can the weary or storm-tossed spirit find rest. All the precious things, or almost all, that the heart can really care for are there. Among its household words are all the fond terms of endearment that constitute affection's native speech. There the hands that do the toil and wield the power of the world become loving and tender in blessing. There the voices that command the applause of listening senates, or raise the shout among the captains of the world's warfare, become soft and gentle in benediction. There man is seen at his noblest, for there in gracious courtesy and service he acts the king. There woman is seen at her loveliest and best, for there she is what the loving God gave her to man to be, — a helpmeet and a queen. There among the children of the household are to be seen the future rulers and toilers, the thinkers and workers, who are going to make this old world fairer and better than ever we have made it; and in their very laughter and prattle we elders hear the sweeter, richer music of the coming years. But let me hasten on. No words of mine can tell, and no words of mine are needed to tell, the blessedness that belongs to that one dear spot called home. Oh, doubly dear it may be to those who have it not, but only remember its blessedness; and dearest of all it may be to those who look forward to the renewal and the fulfilment of its joy in heaven!

SERMON VIII.

MY NEIGHBOR.[1]

If ye fulfil the royal law according to the scripture, Thou shalt love thy neighbor as thyself, ye do well: But if ye have respect to persons, ye commit sin, and are convinced of the law as transgressors. — ST. JAMES ii. 8, 9.

THE good old word "neighbour" has a meaning of its own that is peculiar to our English speech. Like the word "home," it enshrines a tradition and stands for a history. It has therefore a monumental interest which entitles it to attentive study. It means, as you know, one who, because he lives in a near dwelling or home, is specially related to us; and upon the relation which it signifies there have been builded more than one of the institutions of Anglo-Saxon civil society. From its earliest times among that people the bond between neighbors was so definite and intimate that in the eye of the law one neighbor was held to be responsible for the security and well-being of another. If a man was murdered, the neighbors were in the first instance accounted responsible; and it was only when they had purged themselves by finding and convicting the real murderer, that they were held to be acquitted of their

[1] Preached in Christ Church, Detroit, on the morning of the Third Sunday in Advent, 1885.

responsibility. So also in case of dispute or disagreement between any two neighbors, twelve or more of the other neighbors were summoned as an assize to determine the matter. There is no doubt that it was upon this ancient custom that our great institution of trial by jury was founded; and it is upon the same custom, the same ancient and sacred bond of neighborhood, that what may be called the very corner-stone of our public liberty rests, — that is, the right and the duty of local self-government in all matters not expressly delegated to the national power. If time permitted and occasion required, it might be shown that in making much of this relation of neighborhood, instead of the tribal relation of kindred or clanship on the one hand, and of association of trades or industrial classes on the other, our English civilization early emerged out of the merely tribal state which has generally distinguished Keltic people, and from the first made its protest against all kinds of socialism and its kindred imperialism; and that from the first it formed the unit of civil society in the home, and recognized only those civil bonds that bind the family to those which stand around it as neighbors. Suffice it to say that the result has been the building up of a civilization unique in the world's history, — a civilization in which the liberty of the individual is preserved entire because it is defined on every side by the same limitations of neighborliness that limit and support every other man; that therefore the English-speaking people of the world have always been at once loyal and free, because loyalty has begun at the fireside and has spread thence from neighbor to neighbor till all the nation has been bound together in one bond; and that because this bond has been produced from within instead of being imposed from without, it leaves manhood unimpaired and unfettered by law, and freedom but another name for duty. And when upon this natural relation the vitalizing influence of Christianity was brought to bear, the result has been the formation of that peculiar institution among English-speaking peoples, and especially in our own land, which is called by the name of society.

If, however, we go back of these considerations to first principles, we find that the enactment on which all human society rests is the royal law given by God himself and re-enacted by his Son: "Thou shalt love the Lord thy God with all thy heart, and with all thy soul, and with all thy mind. This is the first and great commandment. And the second is like unto it: Thou shalt love thy neighbor as thyself." This, added to that unwritten law of man's nature called the *societatis appetitus*, is itself the enactment of that social economy which after all these years and in this land of ours is destined to attain, we believe, to its fairest fulfilment in Christian society. There is a singular expression of this royal law as first given by Moses, then re-enacted by Jesus, and finally as expounded by Saint James, which is very significant. In Leviticus, the Hebrew word which is translated neighbor means companion, friend, associate, equal. When Jesus re-enacted it, and His words were translated into the Greek language, the word which is given as neighbor means much the same as our English word, — that is, a *near dweller*. And this larger meaning of the word and of the command Saint James further expounds and enforces when he says, "If ye fulfil the royal law according to the Scripture, Thou shalt love thy neighbor as thyself, ye do well: But if ye have respect to persons, ye commit sin, and are convinced of the law as transgressors." Now, then, taking this royal law as thus expounded, let us see how it enacts the establishment and requires the perfection of that peculiar Christian economy which we call society.

That man should enter into some kind of social relation with those about him, is indeed a necessity of his nature. For he is a social being, and it is only in the mutual amenities and exchange of social intercourse that his happiness finds its completeness. The issue of this natural impulse, unguided by religion, may be registered in friendship, — an attachment to friends accompanied by hatred to enemies. Among all heathen people and all barbarous tribes there has been, therefore, no lack of friendship, just as there has been no lack of savage hate, and the one has usually been commensurate with the other. There is no time now to consider the inadequacy of this natural impulse alone to hold society together. Beautiful and gracious as natural friendship is, it is too limited in its extent, too dependent on the peculiarities of individuals, too frail and uncertain in its tenure, to constitute a basis sufficiently broad and enduring on which society may securely rest. There must be a larger, nobler principle which shall take this impulse and extend its action far beyond its natural limits. And this is to be found in that royal law enacted by God and re-enacted by Christ: " Thou shalt love the Lord thy God with all thy heart, and with all thy soul, and with all thy mind. This is the first and great commandment. And the second is like unto it, Thou shalt love thy neighbor as thyself."

You will observe, then, that love to one's neighbor is here likened to love to God. This discloses the great truth that is founded on it, and is measured by it. Let us try, then, to get at the principle on which love to God must rest, and this will be the principle of love to our neighbor. Why, then, should we love God with heart and mind and soul and strength? It is because in God man finds the ideals which are the prototypes of all that is noble in himself, and which therefore he must love if he would be true to his own better nature and higher destiny. It is in the fact that man was made in God's image that we find his supreme obligation to love God. It is impossible for him not to love such an ideal without turning from his true destiny, renouncing his eternal birthright, abjuring his glorious mission. For man not to love God with all his heart and soul and mind is degradation. For man, whose heart was formed for love, not to love the great heart of the Everlasting Love; for man, whose soul was fashioned in God's image and bidden to aspire to His likeness, not to adore the great Soul of all things; for man, whose mind is the faint reflection of the Divine Mind, not to worship the Eternal Majesty, to whose thought all things are present, — is to be something less or other than a man. It was therefore but the statement of our everlasting truth when Christ said, To do this is the first and great commandment. But immediately he adds, The second is like unto it, and that the two together fill up the whole range of human duty. "Thou shalt love thy neighbor as thyself." Now, then, it is in the likeness of the second commandment to the first that its supreme obligation lies; and this we must consider for a moment, for it is the basis of all Christian society.

The obligation of man to love his neighbor as himself lies in the fact that it is in his neighbor that man gets his clearest revelation of God, — more clear than any revelation in words, more clear than any revelation in works. It is in the soul of man when looked at with the eyes of neighborliness that man gets his best vision of the majesty and beauty of God. Spite of all the defilements of sin, spite of all the disfigurements of selfishness and worldliness, it is in man's regal nature of heart, soul, and mind that we catch our best vision of God. When we begin to look at it in this way, we see that loving men is a religious thing. It is a religious thing so to love men as to delight to meet them and mingle with them in society. To be able to look with open vision on Nature's grand and lovely forms, and to see and love the ideal beyond or behind them, is esteemed a precious gift. So also to find a joy in the flowers, a delight in the morning, a pensive ecstasy in the light of setting suns; to feel with the poet, —

> "There is a pleasure in the pathless woods,
> There is a rapture on the lonely shore,
> There is society, where none intrudes,
> By the deep sea, and music in its roar."

But far above this gift is the precious, the divine gift of loving men and taking delight in their company. To love men as men, not for what they have nor for what they think or know, but to love them because they are made in God's image, and because in them man gets his only open vision of the great archetypal mind, soul, heart, — thought, goodness, love, — oh, this is one of the grand things for man to do! Next to loving God, it is the grandest thing for a man to do; and the supreme obligation to do this is the basis of all Christian society.

Now, then, in the light of these considerations let us think for a few moments — first, of the dignity and discipline of society; then of the educational influence of society; then of the dangers that beset society; and finally of the blessedness of true Christian society.

And first, of the dignity and discipline that belong to it. If we take society now as we know it, the social intercourse of Christian men and women under well-known rules of politeness and good manners, we find that it has a dignity of its own that entitles it to be considered one of the loftiest results of Christian civilization. Society in this sense is peculiar to the Christian nations. The heathen have not and never had anything like it. At this moment there is nothing to correspond to it in China or Japan, in Turkey or Egypt, or in any non-Christian land, just as there was nothing like it in imperial Rome, or cultured Athens, or learned Alexandria. And even among Christian peoples it has been of comparatively recent development. It existed only in the most rudimentary form in the early centuries of our era, and in the Middle Ages. Chivalry was only a splendid prophecy of what it was to be, but nothing more. It was not till comparatively recent times that the great commonwealth of men and women which we now call society was organized in the civilized world; and even now it is only among the English-speaking peoples and their congeners that it has attained a free development. Among the Latin and Gaulish races, for instance, there is such distrust of women, and such jealous restrictions are placed upon her, that the free intercourse of polite society in our sense of the word is impossible. Finally, it may be said that of all the English-speaking peoples, society has attained or may attain among us its noblest form; because here we are free from the degenerating effect of a merely hereditary and titled aristocracy. Society, in a word, is here left free to rest on that great enactment which God has made, which is binding on all alike, and which urges man by the loftiest sanction known to mind or heart to love his neighbor. Hence, we have the great commonwealth of Christian society, — a commonwealth which has its own gentle and gracious laws; its silent tribunals which noiselessly but unerringly enforce them; its dignities, its honors, its joys, its labors, its duties, its delights, the movements of which constitute the characteristic economy of modern civilized life.

Now, the discipline of it will be apparent when it is considered that the one principle which regulates it throughout is self-sacrifice. It is a great truth that the principle of the cross underlies all good manners. Self-denial, self-control, self-sacrifice, the very essence of Christianity, are actually put into practice in the behavior of good society. Men must restrain their baser impulses and instincts. Selfishness, if it exist at all, must at least be dissembled or concealed. Self-assertion must be abandoned. No man can even seem to be a gentleman who does not put into practice those principles of the cross of Christ which the gospel commends to us; and no man can really be a gentleman unless he have those principles in his heart. Therefore it may be said that Jesus was the first gentleman in all the world after Adam fell; and still the only way to become a real gentleman is to take Jesus for a model. The discipline of polite society, therefore, is of much importance in the culture of the Christian life, since it is the actual putting into practice of its principles, which like all principles cannot be fully appropriated until we use them. Therefore it is that the Christian man who moves among his fellow-men in social intercourse is so much nobler, grander a man than the recluse, the hermit, the monk, the dweller in a cloister. The solitary man or woman is almost sure to be self-willed, self-centred, lacking in the finished grace of the Christian life. The monastery, the nunnery, the cloister, the hermitage, are not favorable to the development of the highest Christian character. The best field for the exercise of the Christian virtues, next to the Christian home, is to be found in the walks, the employments, the innocent pleasures, the gracious and generous courtesies that belong to Christian society.

These considerations leave but little to be said of the educational influence of society. As I have already intimated, we learn in social intercourse some divine things that we could not otherwise learn. Nay, we look upon the Divine in the human, and through the human we learn to love the Divine. "If any man love not his brother whom he hath seen, how can he love God whom he hath not seen?" What a book is the mind of man! What a mystery is the human heart! In Christian society we study the deepest mysteries of the human soul, we may bend over the fairest pages of human thought. To see Christian men and women at their best; to turn toward them the best side of our nature; to abjure pride; to banish self-seeking and selfishness; to follow, if only for an hour, lofty ideals; to enjoy the bright flashes of wit, the sustained delight of high converse; to think not of self, but of others, and to lose one's self in gracious ministry to others, — this of itself ought to be an educating, elevating, ennobling employment, which would train man for ideal pursuits both here and hereafter. Ought to be, will be, provided society be kept pure, simple, high-minded, in all respects what it ought to be.

And this brings me to my next topic, — the dangers which beset society. Here again I must be very brief. Time does not permit me even to enumerate more than three of them. These three shall be, selfishness, worldliness, unreality. And first, of selfishness. Enough has been already said to show that selfishness is really incompatible with all good manners, and is therefore the foe to all society. But there is a more subtle selfishness, which, while it does not express itself in unmannerliness, is nevertheless just as really unmannerly. I mean the selfishness which is always seeking its own good, its own advancement, its own advantage, in, through, or by means of society. Surely I need not characterize this base, sordid, ignoble temper or disposition which so abounds in the world, among the poor just as much as among the rich. This it is which so often makes society a mere vulgar competition, hospitality a mere sham and bargain, like the publicans giving merely to receive as much again. Akin to this danger, and no less base and sordid, is the frivolous or calculating worldliness which makes society a mere means of vulgar and pretentious display, — a display which excludes the poor, which alienates classes, which works ruin to many a household, and which like a dry-rot soon makes the society where it prevails a mere sham.

This brings me to the mention of the last danger, unreality. In society it is so easy to be unreal; to pretend to feel more than one does feel; to seem glad when one is not glad, and sorry when one is not sorry; to say smooth and false things, because smooth and false things are so easy to be said. What is the remedy? I answer, a return to the great first principle on which society is founded, — love to one's neighbor because he is a neighbor, the man whom God has given to you to care for; who, because his home is near you, you are related to him; who, because he is a man, a regal creature, made in God's image, in whose nature you can see some vision of God, him, therefore, ye ought to love. Oh, to love one's neighbor, not for what he has, not for what he thinks or knows, not for what one may gain by it, but to love him because he is a child of God, — this is the royal law, the keeping of which is to be royal, to do well! Oh, if our men and women could only rise up to the height of this great argument, then indeed would society be purged of all its meanness and frivolity, and guarded from the manifold dangers which beset it! Society would simply be Christianity in its holiday attire, — none the less pious, none the less faithful, because joyous and glad. "Therefore, love is the fulfilling of the law." If there be any other commandment, it is briefly comprehended in this saying, namely, "Thou shalt love thy neighbor as thyself."

More than two thousand years ago there lived a sage in a far Eastern land. The people of his nation were rude and barbarous; the days in which his lot was cast were very evil. The great thought rose up in his heart that he would redeem the time and save his people. But he knew not God. He only knew man, or as much of man as one who is without the thought of God can know. So he took the half-truth which he did know, and upon it he constructed his great philosophy. He made religion to consist altogether of good manners; and to this day one third of the human race venerate the sage Confucius and accept his philosophy. Let us not deride the great Chinese philosopher. He was not altogether wrong. He was partly right. The only secret of his error was that he did not know God, and hence he could not base his noble precept of love to man on the only secure foundation on which it can rest, and that is love to God. Five hundred years later a greater than Confucius arose,—one who out of the richer treasures of His thought brought forth all wisdom and all knowledge. He supplied what Confucius lacked, and in likening love of man to love of God, He disclosed the twofold principle of all religion and all society. His familiars and His apostles understood Him. They learned the mighty secret of all religious, of all social, of all political development, as they sat at His feet. Ages passed on,—ages of barbarism, cruelty, wrong. Slowly, surely, the great principles which he enunciated have won their way. At last they are finding in this age, in this land, as I believe, a fuller, richer development than ever before. We see, with all the faults and shortcomings of our time, that there are men and women who do love God, — and oh, how that love ennobles them! — and do love men because they love God. This love of man is now organized into a great economy; but many are using it mistakenly, selfishly, falsely. The question, then, constantly arises, What is the principle on which this new economy of social intercourse ought to rest? I turn for an answer to the words of the great Master. I read the exposition of that answer by the apostle James, who sat at His feet, and who calls it the royal law. And then for the definition of that sufficing, supreme love to God and man which is the code at once of all religion and all society, I turn to the writings of the great apostle. Thou shalt love God, and therefore thy neighbor, said Jesus. And Paul the apostle expounds that love. Listen to it. Here is at once the code both of religion and good manners. "Though I speak," he says, "with the tongues of men and of angels, but have not *love*, I am become sounding brass, or a clanging cymbal." This, then, is the principle which makes a man at once a gentleman and a Christian; this is the royal law: "Thou shalt love the Lord thy God; . . . thou shalt love thy neighbor as thyself."

SERMON IX.

BUSINESS.[1]

And that ye study to be quiet, and to do your own business, and to work with your own hands as we commanded you; That ye may walk honestly toward them that are without, and that ye may have lack of nothing. — 1 THESS. iv. 11, 12.

THERE is a word which has come to mean much in our daily speech, — whose meaning as we use it cannot be expressed by any single word in any other language, — and that word is "business." Like "home" and "neighbor," it enshrines a tradition and stands for a history. There is not time now to follow the development of the word and its signification, until, as at present, it means a vast department of human activity, in which all the movements of labor and commerce are included. It now stands for a far-reaching estate, which, though it cannot be claimed that the Anglo-Saxon race created it, has undoubtedly been organized by English-speaking peoples, who have made it the controlling power in the modern political world. The old sneer that the English are a nation of shopkeepers has lost its point, though not its truth. More than all other secular agen-

[1] Preached in Christ Church, Detroit, on the morning of the fourth Sunday in Advent, 1885.

cies, the business enterprise of the English-speaking races has blessed the human race. It has led the van in the triumphal progress of Christian civilization. It has opened up continents, peopled deserts, and whitened solitary seas with the sails of commerce. Therefore the old English word "business" has come to have a definite and noble meaning. It stands for a mighty commonwealth wherein men and nations are intimately related to each other. It has its own laws, enacted by the Supreme Law-giver, which senates and parliaments do not need to enact and cannot set aside. It enforces these laws by the swift and unerring awards of success or failure. It builds its own capitals in many lands on spots designated by God himself, and in them it erects stately palaces which far outstrip the pride and magnificence of former ages. It has its own leaders, and it sets one up and pulls another down according as each obeys or disobeys its behests. Kings and cabinets are obedient to its commands. Armies are now little more than its auxiliaries, the hired mercenaries with which it protects its interests. A monarch surrounded by Oriental pomp in his Eastern capital dares to interfere with the interests of a lumber company in Burmah. An English expeditionary army sets out from Calcutta, marches to Mandalay, dethrones that mad and foolish king, and sees to it that the injured lumber company shall cut their logs of teak on the mountains of Burmah in security and peace. When Muscovite or Austrian ambition marshals its legions, or Moslem fanaticism musters its Asiatic hordes, the business interests of Europe and the world call a halt to the fierce armies, and insist that peace shall not be broken, nor war declared except as they shall dictate. The success or failure of campaigns, of diplomacy, of statesmanship, is registered instantly, in all the world's markets, in the rise or fall of prices, in the establishment or impairment of business confidence. And so it has come to pass that almost all the practical concerns of the world have fallen under the influence of its potent mastery, and yield to the demands and movements of business.

When we go behind these general considerations, however, we find that this great commonwealth rests on God's enactment. When He commanded man to replenish the earth and subdue it, He issued His royal charter to business. Business means the appropriation and subjection of the world by man to himself. Beginning with agriculture, which is its simplest form, and rising through all grades of industrial and commercial activity, whatsoever subdues the external world to man's will, and appropriates its power, its beauty, its usefulness, is business; and whoso worthily engages in it is helping to carry out God's design, and is so far engaged in His service. To conquer the earth, and force the wild fen or stony field to bring forth bread to gladden the heart of man; to level useless hills, and say to obstructive mountains, Be ye removed from the path of progress; to summon the lightnings to be his messengers, and cause the viewless winds to be his servants; to bring all the earth into subjection to human will and human intelligence, — this is man's earthly calling, and history is but the progressive accomplishment of it. Therefore it is, that, rightly regarded, business is a department of Christian activity. Therefore it is to be said and insisted on, that the worthy business of every-day life is a department of genuine Christian culture that ought to be pursued with high aims and lofty motives, not only for what it enables man to do, but chiefly for what it enables man to be in the exercise of his kingly function and in the development of his kingly character.

Let us think, then, for a few moments this morning of the disciplinary and educational function of business, and of some of the dangers that assail those who are engaged in it. The apostle, in commending men to faithful diligence in business, names two motives which undoubtedly have played an important part in controlling and encouraging men, — " that ye may walk honestly toward them that are without, and that ye may have lack of nothing." To supply one's daily need, and to make and keep an honorable place in the world, may not seem to be very lofty motives; but they are, at least, universal in their operation, and of daily urgency. Because men need food and clothing and shelter; because they desire for themselves and their children comfort, security, plenty; because the mind craves books and painting and music, and all the elegances and delights which money can buy; and because the aspiring heart craves the respect and admiration of its fellows, — these are motives which have sufficed to make some men toil in all ages. But in this land, of all others, these motives have asserted their power as nowhere else, and made our people a nation of workers. The intelligent foreigner who comes to our shores is struck with the anxious, eager look on men's faces. All life is eager, active, few or none despairing of rising in the world, and fewer still content with the fortune to which they have already risen. Everything partakes of this restless, feverish energy. Agriculture, manufactures, very much of professional life even, is possessed and dominated by the commercial idea of getting on. The vast majority of our people do, with more or less assiduity, attend to their own business, desiring to walk honestly, or honorably, toward them that are without, and to have lack of nothing.

Now, whatever we may think of the motives which underlie this fact, the fact itself is far from discouraging. At all events, our people are in earnest about something. They are delivered for the most part from the sottishness of self-indulgence. They have not lost their manhood in the slavery of sensuality. Whatever their motives may be, they are actually practising daily and hourly the Christian virtues of faith or foresight, of prudence, of self-control, of self-denial, of temperance, of uprightness. The characteristic virtues of the business world are Christian virtues every one, and in adopting them men have acknowledged the excellence of Christianity. Self-indulgence is recognized as folly, as the foe to all happiness and manliness. Self-denial, self-control, is known in the practical affairs of life to be the condition of all success. Thus far, then, men have learned the great lesson of the cross, and have taken its principles to be the rules of business life. Therefore it is that if rightly and wisely conducted there is no better discipline for the formation of character than business. It teaches in its own way the peculiar value of regard for others' interests, of spotless integrity, of unimpeachable righteousness; and the busy activities of life, in themselves considered, are good and not evil. They are a part of God's great work, and are as much His appointment as the services of praise and prayer. I think we all need to be reminded of the dignity and sacredness of a worthy every-day life. God's kingdom includes more than the services of the sanctuary. The court-house is his temple too, and so is the chamber of commerce. It is just as holy a thing to work as it is to pray; and the distribution of commerce, the helpfulness of trade, the feeding and sheltering of those belonging to you, and all the honorable ministries in which a high-minded business man engages, are just as truly a part of God's service, if men could see and feel them to be so, as is the function of the preacher. I am not here to condemn these things, or to deprecate men's earnestness in the pursuit of them; but I would deepen and enlarge that earnestness. I would say with the apostle, Study to do these things faithfully, earnestly; but then I add, as he never failed to teach, these things are means, not an end. Their value lies not in themselves, but in the discipline, the character, the power which they give to do higher things.

The warning is not needless. And this brings me to name one or two of the great dangers that beset the man of business. Though beyond all question the business energies of the age have been reinforced and guided by the Gospel, until discipline, temperance, and self-control have become their permanent characteristics, and though beyond all question the business pursuits of the age are recognized by Christian thinkers and economists as departments of human culture and as part of God's administration of the world, yet business men, with all their earnestness and sagacity, are peculiarly liable to be blind to these high considerations and ignorant of this great economy. There are two dangers by which they are continually liable to be betrayed: one is selfishness, and the other is worldliness.

Now, it may seem a trite thing to say, and yet it is not always taken into account, that a business man is peculiarly liable to a special form of selfishness. It is not the selfishness of ease or self-indulgence, as we have seen; but it is the selfishness of gain, of profit, of personal advantage. Profit, of course, is the very essence of success in business. It is the measure of success, and there could not long continue to be business without it. Yet the making of profit is apt to become an absorbing passion with the eager business man for its own sake. His ordinary relations with men are apt to be more or less controlled by it. He is in danger of carrying it into his social life, — of valuing men and policies and principles according to the advantage that may accrue to him from his connection with them. Such a man pretty soon begins to wish to make his association pay, and his friendships, and his politics, and everything that he is and has and does. And if he is successful, a certain selfish pride establishes itself in his heart. We all know this ignoble type of character. And then dogging the heels of this selfish pride comes avarice, — that amazing and monstrous passion of the soul which loves money for its own sake, which grows on what it feeds on, which never can be appeased, which never has enough. Woe to the man who sinks into this slavery! And yet how many men there are who sink into it almost unaware! A young man begins life strong, temperate, self-denying, full of energy and of courage, thinking high thoughts, cherishing noble ideals. He goes into business. The excitement of it pleases him, the success of it fascinates him, the gain of it begins to cast its spell about him. Now, mark how such an one sinks into its toils. First he gives up the Sunday school. Then his place in church is empty. Then he steals off to his office and counting-room on Sunday. Then he gives up old friends one by one. He no longer cares for society. Men praise him for his energy and success. Then he begins to get more and more mercenary, but men still praise him; more and more hard, but men still praise him, until the accursed thirst for gold becomes the one passion his life. Then he does not much care whether men praise him or not, and soon he becomes an Ishmaelite,— his hand is against every man. To say nothing of the hardened and sordid character that this gives him, it defeats his career as a business man. The apostle says, "Be diligent in business, that ye may walk honorably toward them that are without, and that ye may have lack of nothing." This man no longer cares to walk honorably toward them that are without, and has lack of everything.

But how much wiser, even from his own point of view, it is for the man of business to guard against this danger and resist it. To say nothing of the deliverance of his soul from the bondage and degradation of avarice, how much more would his very money be worth to him, if he should heed and obey the gospel! How much larger his success, how much freer, nobler, more worthy, more happy his life! His success would be larger as he went on, and would mean so much more to him. For the miser becomes a coward and loses heart. His selfishness makes him short-sighted, and turns all men against him. But the Christian man of business not only succeeds in the exercise of the Christian virtues, but success means something noble to him. And money is power in the hand of a good man, and he gets more good than he gives, even, in making a right and generous use of it.

But let us thankfully confess that this danger is not so rife as it once was. Our modern life is so full of demands on the profit of business that there are not so many miserly men as there once were. But there is another danger that was never so prevalent as it is now. This may be called the worldiness of business. Men are simply absorbed and engrossed and satisfied with their business pursuits and business interests, and so neglect and forget their religious and eternal interests. I here speak of business as a vast department of human culture, in which man appropriates what is external to himself. If this world were the only world and this life the only life, then it might be wise and worthy in man to devote himself without reserve to the things that belong only to this world and this life. But man is more than a denizen of this world. He is more than an animal to eat and drink and be clothed. He is more than a calculating machine to puzzle over life's problems. He is more than a mercenary recruit drafted into the world's great army to fight its battles of progress. His own spirit bears witness to its immortal dignity and destiny. His heart, which cannot be satisfied here; his reason, which soars above the things of time and sense; his conscience, which bids him look for an eternal retribution on wrongdoing, — his whole nature pleads trumpet-tongued against the shame and indignity of mere worldliness. And yet with strange inconsistency multitudes of business men make light of the wants of their immortal souls, and go their ways engrossed by utter worldliness.

Yes, they go their ways, but their ways are not ways of pleasantness, their paths are not paths of peace. For there is a hunger of the heart which nothing but God can appease; there is a thirst of the soul which nothing but God can satisfy. "That ye may walk honorably toward them that are without"! What can give this, spite of poverty or wealth, but the Christian conscience which is void of offence toward man and God? "That ye may have lack of nothing"! What can assure this but the spirit of adoption, which bears witness with our spirit that we are children and heirs of God?

And now, to bring this Advent series of sermons to a close, we have seen that Christianity has made our homes, our society, our business; and Christianity alone can preserve them. In this fair land, in the midst of this Anglo-Saxon civilization, these institutions have reached, under the influence of Anglo-Saxon Christianity, their fairest development. And what a noble discipline they afford, what a worthy training they give to fit a man for the employments, the dignities, the blessedness of eternity! It is this thought that gives them all their real dignity and all their real value. The one thought that redeems this world from insignificance is the thought of another. He only can live worthily here who is preparing to live forever hereafter. Dear then as our country is, we love it more, the more it grows like the heavenly country. Dear as home is, it is dearest of all when it is most like our heavenly home. Joyous and glad as society is, it is most joyous and most glad when it grows like the society of the redeemed, where there shall be no more sin and no more curse. And business is worthy of man's immortal energies only when it secures for him and those whom he loves the true riches. Men and brethren, to guard our country, to hallow our homes, to purify and elevate society, to ennoble business life and make it more worthy, this is the function of Christianity, — the sober, ethical, practical, home-building, society-fostering, business-encouraging Christianity of this beloved Church, which directly or indirectly has been the source of all that is best in our civilization, which will lead us on, I do not doubt, to still more glorious things in the future, but only on condition that it continue, and even in larger measure, to ennoble our business, to purify and elevate our society, to hallow our homes. And this it can do for us and our children only as it ennobles, purifies, hallows our hearts and our lives.

SERMON X.

REPENTANCE.[1]

> From that time Jesus began to preach, and to say, Repent: for the kingdom of heaven is at hand. — St. Matt. iv. 17.

THE young Prophet of Nazareth had but lately emerged from obscurity. His human soul, we may reverently believe, had but recently appropriated fully the consciousness of His Messianic character. On the banks of the Jordan He had been saluted as the Christ in the midst of thousands of His countrymen, and he had been owned and blessed by His Father's voice out of heaven. Rapt away by the Spirit into the wilderness, He had meditated His great career amid the silences of Judea's lonely hill-country, and had won His three-fold victory over the tempter. And now in the meek majesty of His Messiahship, and with heaven and its ministering angels around Him, He returned in the power of the Spirit into Galilee, and began to preach His gospel. And this was the message which He uttered: "Repent: for the kingdom of heaven is at hand."

We would naturally suppose that the first recorded word of Jesus' preaching would mean much.

[1] Preached in St. Paul's Church, Detroit, on the morning of the first Sunday in Advent, 1886.

All the circumstances that preceded its utterance, and all the characteristics of the preacher, would lead us to believe that in this living word His pent-up soul had found free deliverance. It was the beginning of a matchless career in the annals of prophetic eloquence. Here for the first time the unrivalled orator, who spake as never man spake, opened the lips that were full of grace and truth. A new era in the history of souls had arrived, when the night of old oppression and hoary wrong was to be succeeded by the morning of gladness and peace. And He whose coming was the ushering in of the age of gold, stood forth and spoke with golden mouth His first word, — a mighty, wonder-working, age-transforming, world-awakening word. For when we come to examine it, we find that all our expectations concerning it are more than realized. It was, indeed, the mightiest word that even Jesus ever uttered, and still it resounds through the world like the peal of a trumpet, seraph blown, calling men in this solemn Advent season to newness of life. By a singular infelicity this first word of Jesus has been completely mistranslated in our English Bibles. Because of certain tendencies, philological, theological, ecclesiastical, which there is not time now to specify, the meaning of Jesus has been forced into a Latin derivative word which is far too narrow to contain it. Suffice it to say that the Greek word which we translate "repent" means far more than that term can possibly convey. It means, be changed in your mind; awake to a new sense and a new apprehension of things; take on a change of mind in thought, in will, in heart.

This conclusion of verbal exegesis, in which all Biblical scholars are now agreed, is confirmed and illustrated by the context. The reason which Jesus gave why men should awake and be transformed in their minds is this, " The kingdom of heaven is at hand." The conjunction of ideas here is very remarkable. Manifestly something more or quite other than the penitence of mere terror is here enjoined. The nearness of the kingdom of heaven, which Jesus announced, was not a matter of dread, but of rejoicing. It was the advent not of wrath, but of mercy; the coming not of war, but of peace. The heaven to which he pointed was no Olympian realm of warring and blood-stained deities, but the reign of the righteous and pitiful Father, the holy and loving Lord; and therefore His first word was not one of rebuke, but of aspiration, — Awake, be changed in your minds; "for the kingdom of heaven is at hand." It would have been easy for our Lord to have made His first appeal to men on other grounds. He might have begun by directing their attention first of all to the wretchedness and guilt of the lower life. Instead of pointing, in the first instance, to the nearness and blessedness of heaven's kingdom, He might have pointed to the actual woes of the devil's kingdom, in which the whole world was lying in wickedness. He had but to look around Him for the ghastly sanctions of such an argument. Sin, like a stalking pestilence, had wrought universal desolation. Everywhere "indignation and wrath, tribulation and anguish," were visited on the souls and bodies of men, for all had done evil. The vast unnumbered mass of men were groping in hideous darkness. For the millions who tilled the fields, and reared the monuments, and made the roads, and did the world's toil, and fought the world's battles, life was but a season of dumb and inarticulate woe, ended by the rayless, hopeless night of death. Even more pitiful was the case of those who lorded it over the *ignotum vulgus;* for, pursuing pleasure, they found only weariness, and, hungry for joy, a fruitless longing consumed their hearts. Then, as ever, the so-called gladness of selfish worldliness was but a hollow mockery, and all the trappings of worldly pride were but the livery of despair. With what startling emphasis, then, the young Nazarine might have pointed to the Gentile world dying in slow agony before their eyes, and have said, " Except ye repent, ye shall all likewise perish."

He might have said this as His first word; but He did not. He rather pointed men, in the first place, to something better. His way of moving men to forsake the woes of sin was by pointing them to the beatitude of holiness. Be changed in your minds; take on a new mind; "for the kingdom of heaven is at hand." And, oh, friends, this has ever been the Divine way. Whenever God calls men to repentance, He begins by awaking the mind to nobler thoughts, by kindling better aspirations in the heart. The prodigal comes to himself and remembers. It is the memory of something better, even the Father's house, that reveals his present wretchedness. It is the Master's gracious bounty in filling Peter's net that moves him to confess his sinfulness. It is light from heaven that arrests Saul's mad career as he journeys to Damascus, and a voice speaks to him with Divine tenderness out of the excellent glory. So everywhere men are best moved to true repentance by the sense of the gracious nearness of the kingdom of heaven.

Now, then, having cleared the way, let us study a little more closely the nature of that mighty movement of the soul which in our English Bibles is called repentance. Among divines it is considered as consisting of three processes, — illumination, contrition, emancipation or enfranchisement. Let us think of these for a few moments in their order. And first, repentance is the illumination, the enlightenment, the awakening of the soul to the reality and nearness of the kingdom of heaven. Adopting for our present purpose the terminology of the text, there are two kingdoms apprehensible by man in this state of existence, — one we will call the kingdom of the world, the other the kingdom of heaven. The two kingdoms are not distant one from the other; no walls divide them, no sentinels pace their boundaries. There is much that is common to both, however different the estimate or value that is set upon it. The same fair earth, with its trees, its rivers, its hills; the same holy dawns and solemn sunsets; the same sun and moon and stars and revolving seasons; in large degree, the same human interests and pursuits, the same tendernesses and affections of the human heart. And yet so diverse are these two kingdoms, that it is altogether possible, nay it is easy for a man to know almost everything about one of them, and to be absolutely ignorant, insensible, unconscious of the other. Let me try now to make this plain. You all know what I mean by the kingdom of this world. Let us call no hard names, but let us take it at its best. Let us take a man of the world, not a reprobate or an outcast, but a man of intelligence and refinement, one of the best of his class. He looks out on this world with acute and intelligent observation. He engages heartily and prosperously in its pursuits. He takes a thoughtful interest in its manifold activities. He is a merchant, and he studies the laws of trade; he is a lawyer, and he masters the science of jurisprudence; he is a politician, and he knows how to touch the springs of human action; he is a statesman, and he understands the laws of national honor and greatness. Nay, he is a student, a scholar, an adept in the love of science. Art is his pastime; the book of Nature engages his serious thought. He can weigh the planets, number the stars, appoint a rendezvous for the wandering comets; he can tell you how mountains waste and grow, and how continents sink and rise; he knows much about the philosophies and economics of life; he will tell you that sin is foolish when it is vulgar and does harm; that selfishness is evil when it is coarse and unrestrained; that passion is hurtful unless it be carefully bridled; that temperance is the handmaid of pleasure; that moderation is the secret of real enjoyment. Nay, he is so wise, so prudent, so gracious, that he is fitly called a man of the world because he so thoroughly understands the world and its life.

Is there anything, now, that this man does not know, or is not in the way of knowing? Yes, much. There is a whole world, a kingdom all around him, of which he is absolutely unconscious. Perhaps he once knew it, but the knowledge of it has vanished from him somehow. As a child, he lived in it; for, as the poet well says:

> " Heaven lies about us in our infancy!
> Shades of the prison-house begin to close
> Upon the growing boy,
> But he beholds the light, and whence it flows,
> He sees it in his joy;
> The youth, who daily farther from the east
> Must travel, still is Nature's priest,
> And by the vision splendid
> Is on his way attended;
> At length the man perceives it die away,
> And fade into the light of common day."

So, I repeat, the unbelieving man of the world becomes unconscious of the kingdom of heaven. Though men tell him about it, he does not take it in at all. It is all an unreality to him. In vain you tell him that the kingdom of heaven is the real world in which all spiritual greatness and blessedness are, — it is a phantom to him; that its sovereign is the good and gentle God, — He does not acknowledge Him; that it has its own code, — he refuses to study it; that it has its own culture, called worship, — it is foolishness or weariness to him; that it has a whole set of motives and aspirations which in all lands have been the inspiration of all that is best in human history, — he answers with a smile of incredulity or a sneer of contempt when you talk thus to him. In a single word, here is God's great kingdom, even the kingdom of heaven, at hand, and he is blind to it, seeing, with all his intelligence, only what a brute of equal intelligence could see, and loving only what a brute of equal taste could love.

But suddenly and gradually a light breaks in upon his vision. In a whisper or in a trumpet peal the mighty word steals or resounds through the chambers of his soul: Awake, take on a new mind! There is a kingdom of heaven, and it is at hand. Who can tell what the occasion may be when this living, wonder-working word may arouse him? It may be at some pentecostal outpouring, or in some moment of lonely dejection. It may be in the midst of some worshipping throng, or when, in the night's still watches, the jaded or disappointed heart sobs its longing and unrest. It may come like the wail of a lost hope or the memory of a mother's prayer. At all events, the ear does catch the mighty word; and suddenly or gradually he does become conscious that the kingdom of heaven is at hand, — a kingdom not of this world, and yet embracing this world; a kingdom of righteousness but of love, of holiness and therefore of peace; a kingdom whose king is the all-loving Father of men; a kingdom whose strange unearthly code reads in this wise : " Blessed are the meek, blessed are the poor in spirit, blessed are the merciful, blessed are the peacemakers, blessed are the pure in heart," — where they that mourn are comforted, where they that are maligned and evil-entreated are sustained, where the hunger and thirst of heart are satisfied; a kingdom whose symbol of the cross, once so despised, is now sure to represent the very principle of all real wisdom and all real power, even the wisdom and power of God. Illumined by this knowledge, he begins to see all things in a different light. Transformed by this vision, his mind begins to take new views of the world and of life. Suddenly and gradually the mighty word arouses him at last. He sees, he feels, he knows that the kingdom of heaven is at hand.

The next process is known as contrition, the sorrow of an awakened soul at the sense of its exile and degradation. Not a base terror, not a sordid dread, but the noble sorrow of one who mourns because he has been and is unworthy of his true lineage. Oh, it is the homesickness of the soul, the upbraiding memory, which visits the prodigal's hungry and forsaken heart! And then suddenly or gradually more and more of the wonders of that heavenly kingdom are disclosed by the revealings of the Spirit. For the prodigal then is welcome, for sin there is healing, for guilt there is atonement, for restlessness there is peace. And so finally, the awakened, contrite soul turns away from the base servitude of the world, and girds up its loins to go and claim its heavenly inheritance. It renounces the base bondage in which it has hitherto been held, and acknowledges its allegiance to the kingdom of heaven.

My brethren, need I remind you that this great business of repentance is one in which man does not act alone? The illuminating, sin-convincing, energizing power is a power from on high, even the Spirit of God. Nevertheless, because man may resist or yield to the ever-pleading Spirit, it is the soul's achievement also, and it is its noblest act, its most heroic achievement. When from the blue skies of Castile and Arragon the morning sun kissed the returning sails of the storm-tossed Columbus, it illumined the path along which the great Genoese mounted to undying fame; for he gave a new world to civilized man. But far greater the achievement of that more heroic soul who through repentance has won its way to the new world of God, even the kingdom of heaven. When Copernicus read anew the movements of the stars, and discovered that earth is not the centre, but only one of the starry train which move in rhythmic harmony around the central sun, his name took its place in the bright constellation of the world's sages; but far more sage and wonderful is the discovery which the soul makes, through repentance, that man's home and centre is not here, but that all his true interests move around the Sun of Righteousness. When great liberators and emancipators like Washington and Lincoln arise, to strike the shackles from the slave and bid the bowed millions stand erect and free, the world fitly honors them, and holds their names in fond and proud remembrance. But far greater that more difficult and therefore more heroic emancipation which through repentance lifts up the degraded soul, and rescues it from the bondage of sin and worldliness, and enables it to stand once more erect and firm in God's image in the kingdom of heaven. Friends, brothers, when one of you shall accomplish this heroic act, the world will haply know little and care less about it; but in that hour your name shall be writ in the Lamb's book of remembrance, and a new thrill of gladness shall roll through all the ranks of those who wait and serve!

SERMON XI.

SONS OF GOD.[1]

> But as many as received him, to them gave he power to become the sons of God, even to them that believe on his name: which were born, not of blood, nor of the will of the flesh, nor of the will of man, but of God. — JOHN i. 12, 13.

IF it were possible for us to read the New Testament freshly, and as though it were altogether new to us, the thing that would strike us most forcibly, perhaps, would be the remarkable prominence that is there given to faith. In all His teaching and in all His works our Lord made faith the one indispensable condition of receiving blessing or help from Him; and to it He never failed to respond with power. Therefore wherever He went His supreme demand was for faith. As soon as the first great word of His preaching had awakened the soul, the next mighty word was spoken: *Believe.* "The time is fulfilled, and the kingdom of God is at hand: repent ye, and believe the gospel." And from that time he made more and more of faith, as though it included all things, declaring that it, and it alone, was competent to secure and appropriate all the good which He had come to give, — healing for the sick, sight for the blind, salvation

[1] Preached in St. Paul's Church, Detroit, on the morning of the second Sunday in Advent, 1886.

for the lost, life for the dead. Nay, the power of the Infinite was declared to be at its command, and all things to be possible to him that believeth. Not less wonderful was the virtue which the apostles and familiars of Jesus ascribed to faith. According to them it is through faith, and faith only, that the soul is pardoned, justified, sanctified, saved; and it is declared in many places and in many ways, but especially in one passage of unequalled sublimity, that it has been by faith that all the world's worthies have achieved greatness and won renown; not by might, nor by heroism, nor by genius, but by faith they "subdued kingdoms, wrought righteousness, obtained promises, stopped the mouths of lions, quenched the violence of fire, escaped the edge of the sword, out of weakness were made strong, waxed valiant in fight, turned to flight the armies of aliens." And in the passage which I have chosen for my text Saint John assigns to faith a function more wonderful still, declaring that faith in Jesus is the transformation, the divine birth of the soul, to which power is given to be the son of God. "But as many as received him, to them gave he power to become the sons of God, even to them that believe on his name; which were born, not of blood, nor of the will of the flesh, nor of the will of man, but of God."

Upon reflection, however, it is easy to see that the prominence which is assigned to faith in the New Testament Scriptures is by no means fictitious or arbitrary, but that it lies in the very nature of things. When Jesus chose it as the cardinal virtue of His religion, and promised to it alone His power and blessing, He did but illustrate afresh His profound and all-comprehending knowledge of man and man's capacity for greatness. For faith is man's characteristic faculty, by means of which he has done all the noble deeds that have adorned his history. I use the accepted language of philosophy when I define it in its generic sense as that function or movement of the soul by means of which man relies on and confides in the unseen, — a function which every man must employ even in the commonest affairs of life, without which he could not, even for a single day, live a rational existence. In other words, man must believe in more than he can see; he must confide in more than his senses can verify; he must exercise a trust in the unseen, which is a genuine movement of faith, or a reasonable life would be simply impossible. It is faith in the beneficent constancy of natural law which hushes the anxious toiler to sleep when the work of the day is done, because he believes that with the morrow the sun shall return in his strength to gladden the world. And in the morning it is faith that sends him forth to his work and his labor till the evening, because he believes that in obedience to natural law he shall surely reap his reward. Faith in truth guides the student. Faith in justice inspires the jurist. Faith in life and its healing power calls forth the physician's skill and nerves the surgeon's hand. Faith discerns the unseen beauty and wakes the poet's rapture, or loves the ideal grace and kindles the philosophic thought, or inspires the artist's dream. Faith in man and his destiny, even though it be but an earthly destiny, guides the statesman's policy or shapes the patriot's purpose as he employs the arts of diplomacy or hurls his embattled legions against the enemies of his country. So in all ages and beneath every sky it has been through faith, and only through faith, that man has subdued kingdoms and wrought righteousness, or done anything worthily and well either in the domain of action or the domain of thought, in the realm of matter or in the kingdom of souls.

Among the recorded sayings of our Lord there is none, perhaps, that is more remarkable than this: "All things are possible to him that believeth;" and yet there is no one of his transcendental sayings that admits of a more obvious verification. Let us now examine this for a single moment in order to understand faith and its power. "All things are possible to him that believeth." That is, as a man's faith, so is his strength; as he believes, so shall it be done unto him. To begin our illustration of this on the lowest ground, a man must believe in anything in order to use it effectively. He must believe in himself in order to make the most and best of his own powers. He must believe in his fellow-men, or he cannot be their guide or leader. He must believe in the cause which he has in hand, or he cannot conduct it or help it to success. And if in addition to this faith in himself, his fellow-men, his cause and its future, he is wise enough to work along the lines of known law, or if, in other words, he has faith in the law which operates in the domain of his endeavor, then all things within the domain of that law are possible to him. When we study history, we find that this is the secret of all human success. Successful men are men who truly believe in the powers which they invoke and employ, and who because they believe in them use them wisely. The difference between men is not so much a difference of brain power as a difference of faith power. Faith is the attribute which makes men heroic and masterful. Men of faith believe in the power which they invoke, in the agencies which they employ; and using them to the utmost, they accomplish results which to an unbelieving man are impossible. Faith, then, is the wielder of all power. It is the achiever of all success, the architect of all fortunes, the winner of all victories. It rules in the camp, in the senate, and in the field, as well as in the house of prayer.

Now, so far as a merely physical or economical endeavor goes, the faith which wins success need not be Christian faith; but it must be a faith which, whether it acknowledges God or not, does believe in and obey the power of God. For instance, take any successful scientist, like Professor Tyndall, for example. He believes in God's physical forces, and he reverently obeys them. Therefore he is able to employ them, and so in the domain of physics and up to the limit of his faith he wields the physical power of God. The secret of his success as a physical philosopher is that he profoundly believes in the rightness and constancy of physical law; and believing, he obeys and rules, and all things within the sphere of its action are possible to him. So it comes to pass that faithful engineers and mechanics and physicists are mighty men. They have not only their own strength, but God's strength too. They make the lightnings carry their messages, the winds and the rivers turn their wheels and bear their burdens. All that the powers which they believe in can do, they can do likewise; for all things are possible to him that believeth.

Now, precisely the same reasoning applies in the region of the spiritual. There, too, humble faith or trust invokes power and wields power. The same temper of mind and heart that makes Tyndall great when dealing with material things, would, if applied to spiritual things, make him great in Christian effort and prayer. If he believed in God's spiritual forces as profoundly as he does in God's physical forces, he could command the angels as he now commands the lightnings, and could not only send his voice from Lincoln to London, but he could send a prevailing petition to the city of God along the golden chain of prayer. For prayer is the Christian's quest, even as labor is the philosopher's seeking. One seeks with lighted torch the mind's delight or the body's comfort; the other seeks on bended knee some peace or grace for the soul. But in both cases it is faith that wins the power and receives the blessing. All things are possible then to him that believeth, but only as he believeth. The kingdom of heaven is revealed more and more, and as it is revealed faith grows; and as it grows it utters its agonizing cry for more growth. "Lord, increase our faith," is the conquering prayer that wins the conquering faith; and still it cries out for more as it goes on conquering and to conquer.

Now, then, we are in a position to understand the wonderful statement of my text. God's gracious and beneficent power has been revealed to men in the person and by the work of His eternal Son. By faith in that Son, man is able to appropriate the kind of power in which he believes, and so to become a son of God. Marvellous as this statement is, it is yet in exact accordance with the universal operation of all living faith; for first it takes on the likeness, and then it wins the power of that in which it believes. It is so in science, and it must be so in religion. It is so in the kingdom of this world, and it must be so in the kingdom of heaven. It is the universal office of faith first to transform and then to energize. Therefore we may read without wonder that to believe in God's Son is to be born of God, and so to win power to be a son of God. Add to this the further thought that this lofty faith is faith not merely in a principle or a revelation, but in a person; that it is confidence or trust not only in what He revealed and taught and did, but in Him who, because He is the Son of God, is the Revealer, the Redeemer, the Saviour; that faith in Him not only transforms into His likeness, but fits and enables the believer to receive favor and grace from Him, even His quickening, life-giving spirit; that faith in Him, therefore, means pardon, peace, justification, and the indwelling of the Holy Spirit, — we begin to see how true this statement must be, that truly to believe in Jesus as the Son of God is to be born of God, and to have power to be a son of God. And this the text declares is the same as receiving him as a personal Saviour, — one who comes to the individual soul as its Enlightener, Redeemer, Saviour. Oh, then, this is the supreme question for me to ask myself, Have I this personal faith in the Son of God, living faith in Him, — not simply in His doctrine, His teaching, His church, His ordinances, but faith in Him? When in my weakness or my wretchedness He comes to me, do I receive Him? Is He my accepted Saviour? Do I put my trust in Him? If so, I am born of God; I have power to be a son of God.

Brethren, let me conclude with two thoughts, — one of comfort, one of warning. To be a son of God, oh, that is the loftiest aspiration of the human soul! Time would fail me to tell how the heathen have missed the way to attain to that sonship, and how men of the world still miss it. It is a secret thought that lies at the root of all ambitions, all dynastic combinations, all aristocracies of hereditary honor and power. But by none of these are men able to attain to that divine sonship which their souls long for. Royalty grows effete and brainless, and often mad. Nobility of birth grows corrupt and shameless, as every daily paper tells. Pride of intellect is not more effective than pride of purse to keep a man from baseness. There is no man but the Christian that can be a son of God. But even among nominal Christians how often is the way utterly mistaken. Men and women so often suppose that it is by doing something that they may become sons of God. And so they set out in the servile spirit of servants. Oh, how anxiously they pray, and give alms, and attend services, and wait on ordinances; but all in vain! No sense of sonship comes to the anxious soul. Listen, brother, sister. It is not by doing, but by believing, that you and I can become the sons of God. Believe; only believe! "As many as receive him, to them giveth he power to become the sons of God, even to them that believe on his name." Let us then go back to this thought, my weary brothers and sisters. It is not an easy matter so to believe. It means the renouncing of all self-trust and self-sufficiency; it means the renouncing of sin and worldliness; it means the simple acceptance of Jesus as the one and all-sufficient Saviour; it means a simple, joyful trust in Him. Oh, what comfort in the thought, — it is not for what I do, or think, or say, but it is because I believe, that I am a child of God.

Then comes the thought of warning. If now I am a son of God, I must act as a son, — not in a servile spirit, but in a filial spirit. I must do my Father's will, and be about my Father's business. Not in order that I may be a son, but because I am a son, I will do all things that He commands me. Here, now, is a test which every one of us can apply to himself. Do I act, feel, live, like a son? Am I about my Father's business, and does my soul delight in that business? If not, what is the matter? Oh, is it not that something is wrong with my faith? Has it not somehow been overborne by selfishness, by passion, by worldliness? If so, then let the Advent-cry once more awaken our souls, "The time is fulfilled, and the kingdom of heaven is at hand. Repent, and believe the gospel." And then the gracious promise is still ours, — our Saviour comes to us this day, the living Saviour, in the way of His own appointing, and as many as receive Him, to them giveth He power to become the sons of God; even to them that believe in His name.

SERMON XII.

HOPE.[1]

> Beloved, now are we the sons of God, and it doth not yet appear what we shall be : but we know that, when he shall appear, we shall be like him ; for we shall see him as he is. And every man that hath this hope in him purifieth himself, even as he is pure. — 1 JOHN iii. 2, 3.

IT is easy to see that this noble passage is thoroughly characteristic of its inspired author; for of all the apostles Saint John was the one who had the deepest sense of the dignity and blessedness of the Christian life. By nature he was an enthusiastic, loving, and aspiring man. It was to be expected, therefore, that he of all others would gain, through grace, the loftiest vision of divine truth, and would be at once heavenly-minded and tender-hearted, known among his familiars both as the son of thunder and the disciple whom Jesus loved. It was in strict consistency with this that he was the one who leaned his young head on the Master's breast at Bethany, and who alone of the apostles dared to stand near the Master at the last dread scene at Calvary. So it was he who dared to see and to tell the wonders that were revealed to his eagle gaze in Patmos, and whose

[1] Preached in St. Paul's Church, Detroit, on the morning of the third Sunday in Advent, 1886.

voice breaks with womanly tenderness as he exclaims, " Behold, what manner of love the Father hath bestowed upon us, that we should be called the sons of God." Once before, in the sublime prologue to his Gospel, he had told of the mystery and the power of that sonship. So here again he takes up the lofty strain, and says, " Beloved, now are we the sons of God, and it doth not yet appear what we shall be: but we know that, when he shall appear, we shall be like him; for we shall see him as he is. And every man that hath this hope in him purifieth himself, even as he is pure."

In this passage there are several topics of the greatest interest presented for our consideration, such as the dignity of the Christian life, — Divine sonship; the progressive development of that life towards its lofty goal, which is likeness to God, of which likeness the beatific vision is to be at once the proof and the fruition; and finally, the hope which sustains and ennobles the Christian on his way. " Every man that hath this hope in him purifieth himself, even as he is pure." In order now to understand the meaning and power of this hope, which is my special subject this morning, let us first inquire concerning the reality of the Divine sonship on which it is predicated, and of the movement toward the Divine likeness by which it is sustained. Is it anything more than a mere figure of speech to say that the Christian believer is a son of God?

There is no need that I should go to-day into those profound but luminous speculations of Christian theosophy by which it can be shown, as I believe, that man before his fall was an actual and recognized and conscious son of God. Suffice it to say that creation was but the revealing of a fact, and man made in God's image and likeness was God's child and representative in this lower world. But then came a great apostasy, in which man fell away from his high estate, in which man lost both the right and sense of sonship, and became a creature of time and the world. In this condition, man the fallen one would of necessity have been disowned and forever disinherited of his righteous Father, had not redeeming love proposed and accomplished a plan by which God was reconciled to man, and man might be restored and reconciled to God. In the fulness of time this plan, which was always meritoriously present to the Divine Mind, was actually accomplished. The everlasting Son, the Revealer and Saviour, became man, in order at once to make atonement and accomplish redemption, revealing the reconciled Father to man, and showing a way and providing the means by which man might regain his lost sonship. The fact is that God is now reconciled to all men. So far as His act and grace are concerned, all men have the right to be sons. But man must appropriate and realize his sonship; and the means by which this is done is *faith*, — faith in the Son of God as the Revealer and Saviour, that heroic act of the soul whereby it makes its surrender to God, renews its allegiance to Him, receives the Son of God, and with Him receives power to be a son.

Now, this great transaction is called in Scripture the new birth of the soul; and the phrase is none too strong when it is considered what is done. In all cases the mighty power which accomplishes it is the Holy Spirit. Baptism is its sign, and faith is its appropriation whereby the man appropriates his sonship and becomes indeed a son of God. This sonship, then, is a real sonship. It is no mere figure of speech. Not only does it rest on eternal facts which are of the most tremendous dignity and significance, but it rests further upon the realization and appropriation of that fact by the soul itself in a transaction which is real birth into a Divine sonship; so that this is a more real than any mere natural sonship, — the spiritual sonship of those who are here called the sons of God.

Time would fail me to speak of its dignity. I pass at once to the progressive development of this character in the soul, whereby its dignity is being constantly enhanced. It has not yet been all revealed. "It doth not yet appear what we shall be." We are moving toward a consummation which has not yet been attained, which is likeness to God. Here, now, is another note of the reality of the sonship. In human relationships the bond between father and son is more and more relaxed as time goes on; in this divine relationship it is just the reverse. The Christian grows more and more like the Father, and shall at last be altogether like Him, and shall see Him as He is. In no respect does Christianity more completely illustrate its divineness than in the way in which it saves men and women from the decay and debasement of age, and makes them grow more and more lovely and loving as they grow older. For in the natural man the reverse is true. Out of religion and out of grace, as men and women grow old they grow less fit to be loved and trusted. I know nothing in all the world more ghastly than the degradation which a godless old age inflicts on the dignity and grace of manhood. Well may the man and woman of the world dread its approach, and seek to conceal its outward handiwork. But the true indignity that it works is not upon the body, but upon the unbelieving soul. One of the terrible things that we learn as we gain knowledge of the world is this, — that the older an unbelieving man or woman becomes, the less good, the less loving, the less kind, the more selfish, the more hard, the more cruel, the less worthy, the less to be trusted, the less to be loved. What a terrible revelation it is! This of itself ought to strike terror to the heart of the man or the woman who has not believed. For oh, there is nothing more ghastly than a godless old age! In childhood there is no unbelief: this is the secret of its loveliness. In early manhood the effects of unbelief are not so apparent and not so desperate. At all events, there are impulses that are unselfish and generous and kind. But in a godless age impulse has perished while selfishness has grown apace, and grasping and cruel greed. How different it is with the Christian, the believing man! Fair as is his youth, yet his manhood and even his age are fairer still. In his case there is growth in grace, and gracefulness and graciousness of character, in tender-heartedness, loving-kindness, and all loveliness of spirit. The marks which age sets upon the brow do but lend an added dignity to him. Though his eye grow dim, yet it has the pensive light of another world. Though the face be seamed by thought or saddened by sorrow, yet it is refined by a gentler, nobler grace. Though the hair fade into whiteness, yet "the hoary head is to him a crown of glory, being found in the way of righteousness." So does he increase in dignity as the years go on, because he grows in love, joy, peace, long suffering, gentleness, goodness, faith, meekness, temperance, — in a single word, he grows in likeness to God.

Now, then, the consummation toward which this growth of the Christian life is constantly moving is complete likeness to God, and the beatific vision; and the hope that this shall be his both sustains and purifies him. "Every man that hath this hope in him purifies himself, even as he is pure." Of the function of hope in general, as a regulative movement of the soul, I have not time now to speak. Any hope will assuredly energize and quicken the life that entertains it. This hope refines and purifies it as well. And first, because this hope is not only before man, but it is above him. In climbing toward it, he must leave all meaner things behind and beneath him. And this brings us to the great thought of the text. The hope of the Christian is the one worthy, enduring hope that is capable of lifting man above the earth and leading him to Heaven. For all earthly and human ideals are too near the man to last him more than a little while. No sooner does he propose one such to himself, and begin to mount toward it, than it begins to lose its excellence as he draws nigh to it, and soon it has no power to hold his affections. There is no imaginable state that he cannot so disenchant except heaven, and no model that he cannot un-idealize except the Son of God. Therefore every mere earthly hope is unworthy to rule a man, and if he have no higher, will at last degrade him; because man is greater than any earthly honor he can aspire to, and greater than the world that he lives in, and greater than all its achievements and glories, — yes, greater than anything except God. Here, now, is the eternal grandeur of Christ's religion. It proposes the only worthy and enduring hope to man. It says to you and to me, "If you will, you may be godlike, for you are the sons of God. And you may be like Him if you will, and see Him as he is." *Sic itur ad astra:* This is the way to the stars. And Jesus, our elder brother, has gone before, and opened the way for aspiring man to follow. Behold they go to Him, out of every nation and every land, the leal, the loving, the true-hearted, even those who believe on His name. One by one they shake off all meaner desires, and lay all meaner purposes down, and as they climb toward Him along the various paths of suffering and of duty, their hearts are filled with a common hope, — to be like Him, and see Him as He is.

"Blessed are the pure in heart, for they shall see God." Surely, "every man that hath this hope in him purifieth himself, even as he is pure." Oh that the age could learn afresh the beauty, the grace, the strength, the blessedness of purity! Do we not need to be reminded of the infinite value of this grace which includes all others and measures all others? Does not the world about us need more than all things else to be taught how precious and priceless, how all-comprehending it is? And not less needful is it that the world should know the great truth that no man can be trusted who does not cherish in his heart some high hope, some lofty ideal which purifies him and keeps him pure. I have tried to tell you this morning what the only hope is that is competent to do that; what the one ideal is which can lead man's aspiring soul and keep his wayward heart true. Other hopes may last for a little while; for a little time some earthly ideal may engage and hold the heart. But the one enduring hope, the one hope that survives all earthly failure, that transcends all earthly success, is the hope of the Christian. The one ideal which always summons man to higher and higher achievement is the Christian Leader and Exemplar, the strong and gentle Son of God. Of Him the Psalmist says, "I shall be satisfied when I awake with thy likeness." Of Him the apostle says, "We shall be like him, and see him as he is." Surely we can say, "He that hath that hope in him purifieth himself, even as he is pure."

In the beautiful legends which tell us of Arthur

and the Knights of the Round Table, one knight is described as the bright and consummate flower of chivalry, the brave and spotless Sir Galahad, — whose good blade carved the casques of men, whose tough lance thrusted sure, whose strength was as the strength of ten, because his heart was pure. It was no fond tale, no idle fancy; for many Sir Galahads have lived since Christ came to show men how to be great; and such are the men who have done all the fairest and gentlest deeds of human history. And sordid and commonplace as the world seems to have grown, the only real leaders of men are the men who like Sir Galahad are high-minded and pure-hearted. The time was when such rode forth in armor to resist the spoilers, and keep the far frontiers of Christendom against the heathen invader. Now, however, they do the less conspicuous but not less glorious part. In every Christian community there are pure-hearted Christian men who are the real champions of right, the warders of all that men cherish and hold dear, — men who are kept stainless and pure by the high hope of their Christian calling; men whose high-mindedness gives tone to our society, who are the real defenders of public safety and domestic peace. These are the true defenders of our country, the unconscious champions of its homes, — men to whose star-eyed vision the Christian's hope has risen, and whom by God's grace it has purified and is keeping pure.

SERMON XIII.

SELF-SACRIFICE.[1]

Hereby perceive we the love of God, because he laid down his life for us: and we ought to lay down our lives for the brethren. — 1 John iii. 16.

THAT man should love God with all his heart and soul and mind has been enacted once and again by the Supreme Law-giver as the first and great commandment; and it is obvious that to do this is to fulfil the law concerning God, for love includes all obligations and embraces all duty. It is a shallow mistake, therefore, to suppose that this law of love is merely a sentimental requirement, demanding nothing more than the play of amiable affections or the easy outgoings of a sunny good-nature. For truly to love is to do all the deeds and render all the service which love requires, up to the full measure of the capacity and opportunity; and though to do this is the delight of the loving soul, yet so to love is the soul's noblest achievement, because it includes all sacrifice and service. But man cannot love God simply because he is commanded to do it, nor even because it is reasonable that he should do it. No

[1] Preached in St. Paul's Church, Detroit, on the morning of the fourth Sunday in Advent, 1886.

matter how strong his faith, there must be something in God to call forth his love; and that something there is, indeed, but it is not the perfection of His being nor the splendor of His state. It is not His wisdom, or His power, or His glory; it is His love. It is by His love that He makes His great appeal to man. "We love him because he first loved us." Now, there are two, and only two, conceivable ways in which God could have made His great appeal to man's love: one is by exhibiting His own love in unceasing bounty and beneficence; the other is by showing His love in self-sacrifice. Now, it is conceivable, of course, that God might have relied on the first method, and that only. He is a God of bounty and beneficence, and He might have called all His benevolent power into unceasing and unvarying action to supply every wish and gratify every desire as fast as it arose, giving to man perpetual sunshine, unfailing plenty, eternal spring and perennial flowers. Man's foolish fancy has often fastened on such Arcadian delights, and he has been prone to say, "How good and grateful I would be if God would only give me all that I desire!" It requires but small reflection, however, to show us that man, being what he is, would not only be degraded by such unconditional beneficence, but that he would be made ungrateful and unloving by it. To say nothing of the failure of such a plan to make him noble and blessed, it is certain that it would also fail to make him even love the Giver. However much we may deplore it and be ashamed of it, it is nevertheless profoundly true, that unstinted beneficence does not kindle and keep alive the affections of the human heart. All the base annals of human ingratitude go to show that nothing is more inevitable than that the recipient of mere bounty, no matter how lavish and unfailing, will not long love the good hand that bestows it. The reason is that mere benefaction is not regarded by the human heart as the token of love. Something else must be added, and that something else is sacrifice. Self-sacrifice is the one token of love which man believes in. The one appeal which always touches the human heart is the appeal of the cross. We all are daily reminded of this. In our homes we all know that it is not the carelessly indulgent father who is best beloved by his children; but it is the self-sacrificing father, — the father who, for the love which he bears to his children, bears the cross in his daily life; the father who shows his love by his diligent and self-denying care, whose life is a life of self-giving and of unselfish devotion. So it is not the foolishly-indulgent mother who has either the best or the most loving children, but the mother who daily and hourly bears the cross in carefully guiding, restraining, teaching, ruling her children; who shows her love by many a self-sacrificing refusal and many a painstaking and self-sacrificing reiteration of precept and mandate, — she is the mother whose children are not only noble but loving, and who rise up and call her blessed. Oh, fathers, mothers, you who yearn not only for the well-being but for the love of your children, take this lesson to heart! It is not by your careless bounty or by your easy indulgence, but it is by your Christian self-control, self-denial, self-sacrifice, that you must show the love that is to win love from your children's hearts. Their little hearts are not to be deceived by foolish, weak indulgences, and if that is all that you have to give them, then do not wonder if they repay you with base ingratitude; for the child is like the man, and can be touched and ruled by no love that does not show itself in self-sacrifice.

It was therefore in accordance with a profound principle of our nature that God chose rather the second of the two ways of showing His love; not by careless beneficence merely, but by self-sacrifice. "Hereby perceive we the love of God, because he laid down his life for us." And this was in strict accordance with His own nature; for it is His nature to show His love in self-sacrifice. Let us now consider for a few moments the great appeal which He thus makes to our love, not only on Calvary, — though that was its supreme manifestation, — but in all that He is and does, showing that He is actuated by an eternal principle which is the opposite of selfishness, and may therefore be fitly called self-sacrifice; and that this heroic principle is the essential characteristic of his greatness. This is the argument made use of by the apostle in the text; it is more than godly, it is godlike, to show love by self-sacrifice.

It is a great thought that in all that God has

revealed of Himself to us, He has taught us that He is love, and that His love is a self-forgetting love. In the august councils which rule His majestic economy, He thinks not of Himself, but of others. Nay, even in the mystery of the Godhead there have been from all eternity the movements of a self-giving love,—the Father loving the Son, and the Son the Father, and with these the co-eternal Spirit also loving and beloved. So God Himself is no isolated and lonely being, self-sufficient in majestic selfishness, but in the mystery of the Trinity of persons which co-exist in the unity of the Godhead, each person, forgetting Himself, pours out upon the others the treasures of infinite affection. Therefore it is that the doctrine of the Trinity is so precious to the Christian consciousness. To it our hearts turn with grateful relief from the cold and mathematical creed that denies companionship in the Godhead. Before all worlds, as we are taught by our holy faith, this lofty principle of the Divine life found its expression in the mutual interchange of affection betwixt the co-eternal persons of the Godhead, each meditating not upon His own glory but upon the glory of the others. If the life of God had not always been such, it were false to say that He is love. Self-love is selfishness; and I say it with all reverence, there had been no room for real love in the Godhead if there had been but one person in God. But the love which is His life demanded from everlasting to be fulfilled in the sacrifice of self-giving. And this is the essential greatness and the essential blessedness of the Godhead, companionship in unity, each person entirely loving the others and being by the others entirely beloved.

But as if this abounding love desired something less strong, more dependent, to be the object of the Divine affection, the created universe was summoned into being. The myriad worlds of space and the myriad orders of Nature were called forth out of nothingness to be the objects of the Divine care. Therefore as one of the fathers has finely and profoundly said, creation itself was an act of sublime self-sacrifice with God. And this is made the more apparent when we remember the generous conditions under which our race was created. God might have made us so that we could not transgress His law. He might have made us so that we must forever be the mere vassals of His will. But no; He desired in His creatures the love of a freeman, not the fear of a slave. In the magnanimity of His generous providence He made man in His own image and endowed Him with the godlike gift of freedom, and therefore with a power truly to love. And even foreknowing that man might fall away from this love, He yet endowed him with such liberty, because His provision embraced the magnificent purpose of redemption. So before the fiat of creation went forth, the council of peace had already been devised between the Father and the Son. The sacrifice of Calvary was already offered and accepted. The love which called our race into being had already yielded the Son to degradation and death, and the Lamb was slain before the foundation of the world. This deed of supremest self-sacrifice was involved therefore in the very act of creation, and by this token God shows that He loves the creation more than Himself. The cross measures all things, even the sublimity of the love of God; for He called creation very good even while He looked down the ages to Calvary. The cross measures all things, even the completeness of that Infinite Love which planned beforehand, out of love for man, to yield up the Son of God. Oh, then, it is at the foot of the cross that we learn to know God, and that He is loved; and it is there that His great appeal is made for our love in return. For there His love is expressed in language which every generous heart can understand, in the surrender of God Himself in utter self-sacrifice. "Hereby perceive we the love of God, because he laid down his life for us."

Now, then, here is the great appeal. It would seem that no heart can resist it which has been aroused through repentance to a knowledge of the baseness of sin and the blessedness of God's love, and has through faith appropriated the meaning of that love and made its peace with God. The effect is to awaken in the believing heart a responsive love, — a love in its degree like God's love. Nay, by the operation of the Holy Spirit His love is spread abroad in our hearts. Now, the movements of this love in the Christian's heart are no doubt feeble and fitful at first. But as the soul grows in grace it grows also in its power to love God; and always, from the very first, it has its own tokens, and produces its own effects in the character and life, by which it may be known. In some of God's servants this love becomes a great and absorbing enthusiasm of the soul. There are some who can truly say with the Psalmist, " My soul is athirst for God, yea, even for the living God: when shall I come to appear before the presence of God; " or with the sainted Muhlenberg, " Who, who would live alway, away from his God; " or with the great Bishop of Pittsburg, a few days before his death, " I long to be with God; " or Saint Bernard, who wrote the beautiful hymn, —

> "Jesus, the very thought of thee
>   With sweetness fills the breast;
> But sweeter far thy face to see,
>   And in thy presence rest.
> No voice can sing, no heart can frame,
>   Nor can the memory find,
> A sweeter sound than Jesus' name,
>   The Saviour of mankind.
> O hope of every contrite heart,
>   O joy of all the meek,
> To those who fall how kind Thou art,
>   How good to those who seek!
> But what to those who find? Ah! this
>   Nor tongue nor pen can show;
> The love of Jesus, what it is
>   None but His loved ones know."

But in all cases, while it may not, and often is not, such a passion as this, yet the love of God is real in those hearts which have come to a knowledge of His love. I need not enumerate all its tokens. They are summed up in the old word "piety," a word of whose meaning even the heathen had some knowledge when they applied it; as, for instance, to " Pious Æneas," as to one whom the gods loved, and who therefore loved the gods. So, but in larger measure in the Christian, piety is the answer of the human heart to God's love, and it shows itself in the reverence which is the habitual attitude of the soul towards God and all that belongs to Him; in the delight which it takes in His worship; in the surrender of the will to His will, and the joyful doing of righteousness; in the fixing of the mind and heart supremely on those things that are lovely, true, just, honest, pure, and of good report. But there is one supreme token of its presence in the soul, to which the apostle continually appeals, and that is brotherly love, — a brotherly love which, like God's love, shall show itself in self-sacrifice. " Hereby perceive we the love of God, because he hath laid down his life for us; and we ought to lay down our lives for the brethren."

My brethren, I am far from denying that there is such a natural grace as the power to love men. Spite of its rarity in the midst of abounding censoriousness, we know that it does exist; that there are men who are born with this divine gift. All the born leaders of men have it. All great men in all ages have been genuine lovers of their kind. Faith in men is one of the unfailing notes of greatness; and so love for men is another. No man can be a leader of men who does not love them. Some men there are, then, in every land who are born with this divine power, and they are born the leaders, the royal souls, the true kings, whether of low or high degree, and men know them, and follow them for good or evil. This power, however, which is given by Nature only to the few, is offered by grace to all. In the heart that knows the love of God a responsive love is kindled which includes man. Not only so, but the Christian lover of men learns how to show his love with power, and always to make it work for good, — not as the easy good-nature of the sybarite, or with the dissembled selfishness of the demagogue, but in the genuine self-sacrifice of a love that is like the divine love in this, that it moves and enables him to lay down his life. "Hereby perceive we the love of God, because he laid down his life for us: and we ought to lay down our lives for the brethren."

What does this mean? Brethren, it means something that you and I can do, ought to do, daily. It is no impossible requirement, it is no grievous commandment. It is simply the easy task of a genuine brotherly love. It means the reverse of selfishness; it means the habitual thinking and feeling and living not for self, but for others. It is to be shown in a thousand ways, — by the self-denial and self-control of gentle behavior and good manners; by feeling sympathy and expressing it, and by feeling kindness and showing it in the way appropriate to each case, but always in accordance with the dictates of a genuine brotherly love. Oh, it means more than bounty, more than lavish giving, more than careless beneficence. It means simply the appropriate conduct and the appropriate speech of one who truly loves his fellowmen, and who is large-minded and large-hearted enough to show it.

Brethren, never was there a time when this truth needed so much to be insisted on as to-day. Business is imperilled, progress of all kinds is impeded, civil society is menaced by the greatest danger that has ever threatened it, simply because men have failed to heed this injunction of the text, and not only to love one another, but to show it by appropriate self-sacrifice. What is needed, in order to adjust all differences between labor and capital, is simply more of the religion of the Lord Jesus Christ, — a religion which shall teach genuine brotherly love to all men, among all classes; a brotherly love which shall show itself in the self-sacrifice of righteous dealing and kind behavior, which is needed just as much among the poor as among the rich; a brotherly love which shall make little instead of much of the accidents of wealth and poverty, and make every man to show a genuine regard for all men in the way appropriate to each. This is the one thing that can settle our existing difficulties, and restore industrial harmony and public peace. Additional legislation cannot do it, nor can all the foolish and vicious devices of communism and socialism and agrarianism, no matter by whom proposed. They are all but the vain attempts to substitute something cheap and easy in place of the old-fashioned practice of self-sacrificing brotherly love, — a brotherly love which is costly and difficult indeed to the natural man, but which ought to be the delight of the Christian; which is the delight of the man whose heart has truly responded to the love of God. And such self-sacrificing brotherly love is mighty among men. For just as we perceive God's love, not because of His beneficence or of His bounty, but because He laid down His life for us, so will men perceive our love for them, and will respond to it, only when we show it by our loving self-sacrifice. And oh, to do the royal part is not to wait for men first to love us, but to love them first! This is the royal way to win men's love, to constrain them to say, "We love him because he first loved us."

SERMON XIV.

THE ONLY GOSPEL FOR THE POOR.[1]

Jesus answered and said unto them, Go and show John again those things which ye do hear and see: the blind receive their sight, and the lame walk, the lepers are cleansed, and the deaf hear, the dead are raised up, and the poor have the gospel preached to them. — St. Matt. xi. 4, 5.

THERE seems to be no doubt that the faith of John the Baptist had begun to falter. To say that it had, involves no discreditable imputation against the character of that eminent servant of God. He was the free son of the desert, and he had lately been cast into prison, — the very child of impulse and inspiration, and yet he had been bound and gagged by the hand of despotism. He was a brave orator and preacher, who had nourished his youth sublime with the promise that he was to be the acknowledged herald and honored messenger of the Most High; and yet he had been arrested by a cruel and arbitrary king, and banished to a remote and solitary dungeon, out of which the voice of his prophecy could be no longer heard; and the young Messiah, whose advent he had heralded, seemed content to have it so. The Redeemer of whom he had spoken to all

[1] Preached in St. Paul's Church, Detroit, on the morning of the fourth Sunday in Advent, 1887.

who waited and wearied for redemption seemed to have no deliverance to offer to him. And so with the longing of a captive soul not yet fully instructed as to the true meaning and scope of Christ's Messiahship, he sent to ask the question of Jesus, " Art thou he that should come, or look we for another ? " The answer was intended, doubtless, to instruct as well as to reassure him. It was no part of the Messiah's mission to forcibly break the bond of temporal authority. To lift up the standard of revolt against even a tyrant's power was not the appointed work of man's Redeemer, but to loose the captives of sin, to minister to affliction and sorrow, to quicken and raise the dead, and to preach the gospel to the poor, — this was and is the appropriate work of the Son of God.

Two kinds of credentials of Christ's mission and character are here declared to have been despatched to the captive John, — the first miraculous, the second moral. There is no time to say more than a word, in passing, of the comparative evidential value of them. Miraculous evidence is perpetually demanded by unbelief, yet unbelief is absolutely disqualified from understanding it. The whole value of such evidence depends upon the condition under which it is employed, and the uses to which it is applied. It is valuable for the purpose of instructing and confirming antecedent belief, especially when, like John the Baptist's faith, it begins to falter; but it is valueless because it is meaningless to an unbeliever. The prodigies wrought by Christ were veritable miracles. They were the indefensible attestations of His divine power. It is not lawful to worship Christ, and it is not possible even to respect Him, unless the wonders which He did were miracles, wrought, as He claimed, by an essential and indwelling Godhead. But, on the other hand, while Christianity is fully committed to a defence of miraculous testimony, yet it remains true that miraculous testimony alone cannot produce religious conviction. Christ's miracles alone, in point of fact, have never done so, and were never intended to do so. They were the outcome of a supernatural life; and unless we grasp, in some degree at least, the meaning of that life, we cannot be taught by them or understand them.

But the concluding words of the text refer to a better, a higher, a more enduring testimony. Far better than the evidence of miracles, even to the instructive understanding, is the fact recorded here: "The poor have the gospel preached to them." Surrounded as we are by an unbelief that is not merely defensive, but is aggressive and daring, the Christian thinker is compelled to defend and vindicate the intellectual and philosophical side of Christianity. To do this is not only a necessary task, but it is one that is worthy to engage and certain to reward the noblest energies. There is no department of human knowledge that may not be successfully laid under full contribution. We may take our stand upon the loftiest summit of modern thought, and summon buried ages from the sepulchres of the past, and each, as its sages and warriors shall walk dimly under review, shall lay a tribute down at the feet of Jesus. We may spread the volume of archæology out before us; we may go to the East and decipher the epitaphs that mark the spot where forgotten empires have crumbled into dust, and to the West where Nature's more lasting monuments lift up to the skies the sign-manual writ by primeval glaciers and immemorial storms. In every region of earth and in every era of history there are to be gathered evidences of the truth recorded in this priceless volume, — that Jesus is not only the world's greatest Teacher, but is also its Saviour and Redeemer. To follow free thought into every field with a spirit of inquiry as free, and to defend the faith at every point of attack, is a part of the unavoidable duty of the militant Church of God. Yet it is not, after all, on these lofty altitudes of thought that Christianity's most cogent and most persuasive evidences are found, but rather in the valleys and along the pathways of common life, and especially in the hearts of the poor. And by the poor, I mean not only the poor in this world's goods, but all the poor in spirit, all the sons and daughters of affliction, all the lowly-minded and hungry-hearted. To them the gospel comes bearing its own mighty credentials. No splendid argument is necessary to commend it when once the human soul becomes conscious of its need. No miracle of power, no messenger from on high, is required to urge its authority upon a broken and contrite heart. Let sickness come, or bereavement, or sorrow, or the shame of self-reproachful penitence, and make the grieved and stricken spirit poor, and then the heart leaps up and recognizes in the words of the gospel the accents of its Redeemer. Scepticism may vex, and heresy distress, and schism rend the Church; but so long as sorrow continues to sadden, and affliction to desolate, and want, whether physical or mental or spiritual, to agonize the human heart, the poor in spirit will continue to have the gospel preached to them, and will hear it gladly. Martha will tell her troubles to Jesus, and Mary will sit at His feet; when sorrow comes both will go out to meet Him; and Jairus will fly to Him to tell Him about his dying daughter; and blind Bartimeus will raise his supplicating cry; and all the mighty multitude of grieved and penitent and hungry-hearted will seek Him, and will hear His gospel when it is preached to them.

But let us get a little closer to our text. The old word "gospel" means, as you know, "good news," "glad tidings;" and the very fact that Christianity has a gospel, or good news, for the poor, is its great credential. In this respect Christianity is unique, for no other system of thought has any such gospel. Let us take the term "the poor" in its ordinary signification. Let us take it to mean the great and growing class of those whose daily life is a perpetual struggle with want and wretchedness. Without accumulated capital of money, or skill, or thought, they must daily front the great and awful problems of life, and must drudge or beg in order to solve them. Heretofore, perhaps, our country has had fewer than any other land of these outcast and disinherited poor, but now they are beginning to multiply with startling rapidity. And of the comparatively poor, proletarian poor, those whose daily lives are a daily struggle with poverty, and who must depend on daily toil for daily bread, why, they far outnumber the rich and even the independent. Considered as factors in the industrial, economical, political life of the nation, they are of immense importance. To the mere economist or statesman, to one who looks upon them simply as a large and growing class, the study of their needs and capacities is of immense and pressing interest. How much more, then, to a genuine lover of his country and of his kind! How vital the inquiry, what living word of good news has any system or any man to speak to the poor?

And first let us inquire, Has unbelief any such gospel? We will suppose, if you please, that Christianity is for the time being set aside, and that free scope is given to atheism to tell all the so-called good news that it has to offer. Accordingly it comes with jaunty air, and proclaims its lately discovered gospel that there is no God, or at least there is none that we can know or need care about; and that there is no future life, or at least no personal immortality. It is true that all this has a certain sinister sound, since it bereaves man of his noblest hope and his loftiest thought, and relegates him to the condition of the brutes that perish; but let us not be too critical just yet. It claims to be good news, and it tells the careless, the gay, the selfish, that there is no God to judge, and no eternity to reward or punish; and perhaps the selfishly gay and careless may rejoice for a little season in this new evangel. But how about the poor? How about the millions of the weary, the heavy-laden, the hungry-hearted? What gospel has this creedless atheism to give to the poor?

Well, let us be perfectly fair, and freely admit all the comfort that it has to give. It has two messages for the poor, and only two: one, the message of the demagogue; the other, the message of the scientific philosopher. And first, let the atheistical demagogue speak his message; it is the new evangel of socialism, of communism, or anarchy. He begins by declaring that all poverty is merely artificial; that it is the result of the greed of the rich and the cunning of the powerful, who make laws for their own advantage. He tells them that property is robbery; that wealth is crime; that all government is monstrous tyranny; that what the masses ought to do, is simply to overthrow government and abolish property, and let all men have all things in common: that such a revolution would do away with poverty. The answer is, that all this is a contemptible falsehood, a shallow lie. Even if he could carry out his scheme and keep men in the condition to which he would commit them, the result would be, not the abolishing of poverty, but the making of it universal. Not only so, but it would make poverty even more wretched than it is to-day even in its worst form. It would level men down instead of levelling them up, and would recommit them to a state of tribal savagery out of which there would be no power to lift and no hope to guide them. If the dream of the communist could be realized, all traces of civilization would speedily disappear. Skill, energy, industry, capacity, would cease to be employed, because the motive to use them would be utterly impaired. All the noblest enterprises would be abandoned, and the grass would grow in our streets. And along with this economical impoverishment there would be the far worse impoverishment of mind, of soul, of spirit. All the sweet ministries which now adorn prosperity, and all the gentle yet strong graces which now dignify adversity, would utterly vanish. Hope would disappear, and gratitude; in the place of these would arise the utterly savage and brutal traits of unreasoning self-will and other selfishness. If, then, the remedies proposed by communism were possible, they would make the poor man's lot not better, but a thousand times worse; they would reduce him and all men to tribal savagery again, and make the fair earth pandemonium, or a howling wilderness, or a waste. Surely this is no gospel for the poor.

But atheism has another message for the poor, and only one other: this is the teaching, not of the demagogue, but of the man of science. He comes forward and says that the present state of the poor man is not unnatural; that it is not only natural, but it is necessary and inevitable; that it is simply the result of that great law of the survival of the fittest, which makes the strong prosper, and the weak and incapable fail and finally die. Well, let us continue to be perfectly fair. Let us admit that there is such a law in Nature as the survival of the fittest. Let us admit that, so far as natural law is concerned, what the man of science says is true, — horribly, hideously, scientifically true; but surely it is no gospel. The truer it is the less of a gospel it is, and the more need there is for some supernatural gospel to come to man from beyond this dreary reign of remorseless law. In point of fact, the unbelieving man of science does not often try to comfort the poor. It is not such as he that builds hospitals, or orphanages, or houses of mercy. But let us suppose that such a man does undertake to proclaim his scientific creed among the poor. We will go with him, if he please, on his round of enlightenment. He enters the lowly abode of poverty. He finds there a man looking with tearless eyes upon the worn and pinched faces of the little ones that are crying to him for the bread that he cannot give; and he says to him, "My good man, your suffering is but the result of the working of a great law of Nature and of society. It is necessary to the progress of the race that the weaker should give way to the stronger; that the fittest should survive, and that you and your little ones should perish; it must be so for the progress of humanity; your comfort is that in some remote future the humanity that then shall be living its little day on the earth will probably be a little happier because you are miserable now. And as for the weak impulse of benevolence that tempts me to relieve your poverty, it would be a scientific mistake; for it can be scientifically demonstrated that the sooner you die and get out of the way the better." This is all that scientific atheism has to say. It has no good news, no gospel for the poor.

Let us turn now to Christianity. What has it to say to the poor? Oh, now we hear glad tidings indeed; now we hear a real gospel! It comes to the poor man with help in its hands and with pity in its heart; and while it soothes and relieves it tells its good news of hope, of love, of life. It proclaims that his poverty and his want and his need belong to an order and a world that is passing away; and that God, the loving God, has another world, — the real world, — in which to redress all the inequalities of this; that God has a whole eternity in which to console the poor, — an eternity of peace for the troubled, of rest for the weary, of joy for the afflicted, when men and women and children shall hunger no more, and thirst no more; where there shall be no more pain, neither sorrow nor crying, for God shall wipe away all tears from their eyes. Ah, yes, this begins to sound like good news indeed, like a real gospel to the poor. We need not wonder, then, that this is chosen as the mightiest credential of Christianity, — this good news from another world and another life. This sanctifies the humblest lot and glorifies the pauper's dying bed; this alone is able to put the light of another world into the dim eyes of the toiling millions, to charm their weariness away.

But again, the gospel of Christianity is not only the gospel of hope, but a gospel of might. Not only does it tell of glory after suffering, but of glory by reason of suffering. It reveals to the sufferer the sweetness of adversity. It casts a flood of light on the dark problems of pain and sorrow, and reveals the cross as the wisdom and power of God. No one but a suffering Saviour could have disclosed this mighty principle,—the wisdom and power of the cross; and under the teaching of this gospel poverty itself is transformed into a training for heroes and demi-gods. It comes to the poor man and says to him, "Oh, my brother, do not repine. Only take your lot as an appointed discipline of love; only take up your weariness, your toil, your suffering, your disappointment, as a cross; only carry them as a burden which your Master has appointed to make you strong. And so out of poverty shall come riches, and out of sorrow joy, and out of labor rest." This, then, is a real gospel for the poor.

But finally, it is good news, the only good news for the poor, even in this world. For it reveals God's fatherhood and man's brotherhood, and it makes that brotherhood real. Oh the blessed revelation of God's fatherhood! Inexpressibly sweet is this good news to every soul to which it comes. To be told that the great Deity who made and rules this world is no careless potentate or cruel tyrant, or remorseless judge, but a Father, all merciful, all pitiful, all tender; and to have Him revealed by a loving Son as a reconciled Father, who for His Son's sake has already forgiven man's weaknesses and sins, — oh, this is the gladdest tidings that ever greeted human ears; this is the good gospel to all men! How much more is it glad tidings to the poor! For the poor man, disowned and outcast it may be, to be told that God is his Father, that he is a child of royal lineage, even the son of heaven's Almighty King, — how does that evangel dignify and gladden and glorify him! It is true that hardships remain, and trials, and sorrows, and burdens; but these do not matter so much to a child of God. It does not so much matter that the son of a king should have to suffer a little hardship, to camp for a little while on the windy hillside, or to clamber for a season over the dark mountains, especially as he is simply journeying home. And this glorious fact of God's fatherhood reveals another fact hardly less glorious, of man's brotherhood, — teaches the poor man himself, that since all men are his brothers, therefore he must love them as brothers. Think how this sweetens the poor man's life within: helping him to love all men, even the prosperous; to be patient with all men, even the selfish and hard; to be kind to all men, even those who are ungracious and cruel, because all men are his brothers, no matter how unmindful and unworthy, and are therefore to be loved by him. Whether the rich heed this gospel does not so much matter; he heeds it, and it sweetens all his life, banishing envy, and bitterness, and hatred, and malice, and all uncharitableness, in teaching him that all men are his brothers, and that therefore he must feel and act a brother's part with them, even as God is his Father, and that he must therefore act a son's part to God. Surely this is a gospel for the poor.

Finally, it is also a gospel for all men; for in a certain true sense all men are poor. You and I, my brothers, my sisters, we too need this gospel, for we too are poor, — poor in our daily want, poor in our perpetual need, poor in the utter inadequacy of all our possessions to satisfy our yearnings, poor in our dependence on one another and on our God. We bring nothing into the world, and we can carry nothing out. So far as this world's riches are concerned, we all must die as we were born, in utter helplessness and penury. And while we are here how utterly foreign to our true life are all the riches that we possess! How true is the old saying of the Master, that a man's life consisteth not in the things that he hath! Hunger of mind, hunger of soul, hunger of heart, — these daily return to us. The mind, the soul, the heart, is continually crying out for more. Where can we find the more that we need and ask, but in God? And as we meditate on these things, behold our poverty becomes plain. And, strange paradox, to *this* both worlds are given: " Blessed are the meek: for they shall inherit the earth;" "Blessed are the poor in spirit: for theirs is the kingdom of heaven."

SERMON XV.

A CHRISTMAS MESSAGE.[1]

In him was life; and the life was the light of men. — ST. JOHN i. 4.

I THINK we all must feel that there is no service so beautiful as that which is appointed for this day, and that music and poetry have cast the spell of their enchantment about us. Not only in canticle and anthem, but also in the matchless poems which are selected as our lessons from Holy Scripture, the Church still shows that the sweet strains of the angelic hymn are lingering in her heart. But our services are more than a burst of poetic rapture; they are more than a divinely inspired symphony of music and song. They embody the most precious truths which God has yet given to man; and we must not permit the exuberance even of Christian fancy to obscure them. We are called to meditate now upon the profound truths which lie at the foundation of all being, and to think of the most sublime doctrines that are connected with the soul's life. Let us not refuse, then, to company with high thoughts this morning. Let us turn to the magnificent passage which

[1] Preached in St. Paul's Church, Detroit, on Christmas morning, 1887.

constitutes the Gospel for the day, and think for a few moments upon one of its statements, — " In him was life, and the life was the light of men."

My brethren, it is a great truth, that Jesus is the one Divine answer to all human questions concerning God. For long ages the supreme aspiration of the best of the human race had been to find some way in which the creature can come to know and love the Creator. Fantastic superstition and grim or pathetic idolatries had long borne witness in every land to this, humanity's profoundest need, and also to humanity's failure to satisfy it.

But in the fulness of time, and in accordance with the other purposes of redeeming grace, God made Himself known in human form, in order that men might know and love Him. The incarnation, then, was the great revelation of God, the revealing of the Infinite to the finite comprehension, and therefore through the finite; the manifestation of Deity both to human thought and human affection in the only possible way, that is, through the incarnate Son of God. And it is one of the aspects of this sublime unity that I wish to direct your attention to this morning. In Jesus we are permitted to look upon the great mystery of life. He declared this of Himself, and His apostles declared it of Him, in terms which it is impossible to eradicate of their deep and literal signification. Saint John says, " In him was life, and the life was the light of men." Saint Peter speaks of Him as the Prince of life, and the Lord of life. He Himself said at Bethany, " I am the Resurrection and the

Life ; " and again, " I am the Way, the Truth, and the Life ; " and the assurance of continuing existence which He gave to his militant Church was founded on the same great claim: " Because I live, ye shall live also." It is in view of this truth that Christian thinkers often make use of expressions which seem mystical and unreal to unchristian apprehension; as, for instance, when they speak of the Son of God as the fount of all being, of His power as the source of all force, of His constancy as the cause of all permanence, and of history itself as the unfolding of His purpose. And however remote these great conclusions are from the present hypothesis of inductive philosophy, they are easily achieved by sober Christian thought whenever it accepts the great truth that as God is the Author of all being, so His Son is the Revealer of all life. We believe, therefore, not as Mystics, but as sober reasoners from truth to fact, that all the phenomena which men call natural are but the revealings of His power; and that beneath the ordinary workings of Nature and the operations of secondary causes the living love and blessed power of the Son of God are energizing and welling forth. We believe that no man can understand the mystery of the universe, nor the meaning of God's word, unless he accepts this teaching; and we look for the day when science, now so mute and sceptical, will come and lay her well-won crowns down at the feet of Jesus. It is only in the light of this luminous verity that we can begin to understand our Lord's miracles. They simply show the everlasting fact,—the Lord of Nature ordering Nature, and the Lord of Life wielding the powers of life. They were simply the signs and tokens that the universe is as truly subservient to His will as it is subject to His law. And if we could only grasp this truth in its fulness, how easily we should discover the deep harmony that exists between Nature and the gospel! We should see that every manifestation of God in His works is but a new beat of His heart; that His successive creations are the putting forth in forms of matter of an abounding and ever-springing life. And we can intelligently address the poet's apostrophe to him: —

> " God of the granite and the rose,
>   Lord of the sparrow and the bee,
> The mighty tide of being flows
>   Through countless channels, Lord, from thee.
> It leaps to life in grass and flowers,
>   Through every grade of being runs;
> And from creation's radiant towers
>   Its glory flames in stars and suns."

But our Christmas teaching invites us to take a more human view of this great subject. It is not so much in the splendor of His Divine power, nor in the magnificence of His far-reaching purpose; it is not in Jesus the orderer, nor in Jesus the upholder, but it is in Jesus the liver of man's human life that He showed Himself to be the light of men. And the light shines for us upon every phase of human experience. When the Word was made flesh and dwelt among us, He began to live a human life. He was not masquerading in a sham humanity; He was not making believe to live the life of a man. When He was born, He was born into a helpless human infancy. When He grew in childhood, He increased in wisdom as in stature, and like all poor and heroic boys He grew in favor with God and man. When He reached the state of manhood, He lived such an every-day life as other men lived, with homely joys and human sorrows, with toil and weariness and rest. For thirty years there was not much recorded of it, and the reason was that there was hardly anything to tell. It was not in the peculiarities of an exceptional career, nor in the eccentricities of extraordinary achievement, that the Divine life that was in Him exhibited its most precious teaching; but it was in the ordinary duties and common vicissitudes of human experience. And though the time did come when His power flashed forth in miracle and prophecy, yet it was not on these that the apostle fastened when he spoke long afterward of the illuminating splendor of His influence; it was not on His works, though His works did avouch His divineness, nor even on His words, though His words were full of grace and truth, nor was it on His intellectual eminence, nor His genius, nor His statesmanship, though in all these respects He was easily the first of the human race; but it was upon the life that was in Him that the apostle fastened his thought. This it was that made Him the great teacher and illuminator of mankind. " In him was life," he said, " and the life was the light of men."

It is now admitted by all scientific observers and accurate thinkers that life is the mystery of all mysteries. We look upon its work in many forms, but we cannot look upon itself. We see what it does through many agencies and organisms, but we cannot exactly define it. We only know that of all the powers of Nature it is the subtlest and mightiest. When it is present, it holds the swiftest powers of destruction at bay. When it retires, they do their wild work of desolation and death. Not only is it mighty, but it is illusive. When we attempt to examine it, it vanishes; when we attempt to bind it or cage it, it is gone, and leaves death in our grasp. Not only is it mighty and illusive, but it is protean. It assumes a thousand forms. The tender shoots spring up side by side in the springtime; one blushes into a fragrant rose, the other grows into a deadly plant, and yet it is the same principle of life. Two eggs are warmed into being in the same nest; the one grows as a barnyard fowl, the other turns out to be an eagle, and soars away to find an eyrie and a home on the mountain-top. Two men grow up side by side; the abounding life of one climbs the heroic path of duty with aspiring feet, the other is betrayed into ruin by the superabundance of his life. Therefore, I repeat, it is mysterious, it is mighty, it is illusive, it is protean; it seems to be outside of all the organisms in which it does its work, and yet to be so modified by those organisms as to take on indefinite variety. By what name shall we call this subtle, this mysterious, this mighty, this protean power? It is often guarded by a subtle intelligence, and yet it is not intellect merely. It is endowed with unfailing intuitions, and yet it is not instinct. It is force, and yet it is more, because there is no correlation between it and other forms of force. What is it? We must still call it by the one word that has no synonym, by the most mysterious name in all the vocabularies of human speech save one: we must still call it *life*. Now, it was the supreme distinction of Jesus, that in Him we are able to see *life* in its original and essential character. This was the supreme distinction that He claimed for Himself: " As the Father hath life in himself, so hath he given to the Son to have life in himself." So here Saint John says of Him, " In him was life, and the life was the light of men." Here now we have this mighty, this mysterious power doing its own proper work. We can study it here; it no longer eludes us. We can look at it in Jesus as He lived the life, the true life of man. Therefore the apostle says of it, This life is the light of men.

What, now, were the essential peculiarities of life as it was exhibited by Jesus, as it shone forth in Jesus? I answer in few words. In Him was an obedient, a loving, a self-sacrificing life. And those qualities — obedience, love, self-sacrifice — were but the phases or aspects of the same character. In Him life was the outgoing of a Divine nature. In virtue of this, it was never of self that He thought. In virtue of this, self-seeking, self-sufficiency, pride, self-will, all kinds of selfishness were impossible to Him. By this power He vanquished the tempter and rebuked devils, and healed sickness and raised the dead. Nay, by this power He vanquished death itself, and burst the bonds of the grave, and returned again to triumphant and eternal life. Here, now, is a study worthy of men and of angels. On this blessed Christmas morning we will not refuse to ponder it. Life in Jesus, — see how it behaved itself; see how it won its victories, not by dazzling achievement, nor by exuberant overflow in prodigy and miracle, but by a law which showed itself in obedience, in self-giving, in self-sacrifice. Among men this supreme characteristic of life had been utterly forgotten. It was supposed that life was a grasping and self-seeking thing; that it was rich and strong and worthy in proportion to what it gained and exacted and appropriated. It was supposed that giving and self-giving were the wasting and abdication of its power; that sacrifice and self-sacrifice were utter shame and defeat. But behold, when the Divine life flowed into the world at the birth of Jesus, and began to do man's part and to be man's life, there was a complete reversal of this human judgment. Then it was seen that life is strong and rich and worthy in proportion to what it gives, what it parts with, what it bestows; that self-forgetting is its health, that self-giving is its joy, that self-sacrifice is its triumph and its glory. Such was the life that was in Jesus, and this life is the light of men.

My brethren, let us not refuse to ponder this

great lesson as we commemorate the human birth of the Son of God. Perhaps there has never been a time when such a lesson was more needed than it is to-day. In this age of a material civilization so splendid as to be almost barbaric, and when human success is rewarded by material achievement, how subtle the danger that we and our children may make the fatal mistake of supposing that life's characteristic excellence and dignity consist in getting and appropriating and heaping up, instead of in giving, in bestowing, in blessing; that we should forget the old divine truth, that he is richest who gives most, and he is most blest who loves most, and that he is strongest who most completely sacrifices himself. Let us seek, then, on this Christmas morning, to cast away our false conception, and return to true views of life. The very story of Bethlehem and the manger contains a correction of all our false thinking. See how completely the very beginning of Jesus' earthly life seems, as we meditate upon it, to teach us true and large and noble thoughts. On this day the Divine life flowed into the world, and began to do man's part in the human life of Jesus. Yet it was an outcast birth, in order to teach us that life is more than the clothes it wears and the house which it inhabits. It was a lonely birth, in order to teach us that life is more than any associates of kinship or companionship that can cluster around it. It was the birth of utter poverty, in order to teach us that man's life consisteth not in the things that he hath. Yes, life is more than houses and dignities and riches; its essential dignity and grandeur cannot be impaired or enhanced by the absence or by the presence of these or any of these; but whatsoever dignity and grandeur it shall have is measured only by the love of which it is the fulfilment. Do you tell me that this is a teaching too transcendental for our day and time? Yet this is the teaching, not of the birth only, but of the whole life of Jesus. Strange contrast between the base and sordid ideas of the world, and the grandest and most heroic life in all its annals! Strange that it must be said of the Divine man, of the ideal man, of the model of all manly excellence and dignity and worth, that He was not a maker of money, that He was not a seeker of dignity or place, that He was utterly homeless, and without a place of His own to lay His head. And yet how strong, how affluent, how glorious was His life! It was the Divine life doing man's part in the world, and therefore it was the ideal life. "In him was life, and the life was the light of men."

Yes, it is a mighty truth, a precious truth, a truth that is needed to save this age from sordid baseness and shame and degradation. Poets have tried to illustrate and embellish it. Sages and philosophers have lavished their thought upon it to give it acceptance among men; but how shall we learn it so well as in the old gospel story, — by simply looking to Jesus. In Him was life: in Jesus the outcast babe; in Jesus the obedient boy; in Jesus the lovely youth; in Jesus the wayfaring man; in Jesus the self-forgetting teacher; in Jesus the pitiful Saviour; in Jesus the dying Redeemer; in Jesus the self-sacrificing and therefore triumphant God. Men thought it was poverty, but the angels knew that it was riches; men scorned it as weakness and shame and defeat, but the angels came thronging through the cloven skies to hymn His greatness when He was born, and they waited on Him and ministered to Him all through His glorious career, and they watched with bated breath the grandeur of His sacrifice, and they told with shining faces of the consequent glory of His resurrection and ascension into heaven. They have always known, and would that we might always know, that "in him was life, and the life was the light of men."